LEARN TO LANDSCAPE

An 8 Step System
That Every Home Landscaping
Beginner Needs to Know to Make
Your Garden a Thriving and yet
Beautiful Masterpiece

LEARN TO
LANDSCAPE

LEARN TO LANDSCAPE

AN 8 STEP SYSTEM THAT EVERY HOME LANDSCAPING BEGINNER NEEDS TO KNOW TO MAKE THEIR GARDEN A THRIVING AND YET BEAUTIFUL MASTERPIECE

THE GREAT GARDENING ACADEMY

© **Copyright The Great Gardening Academy 2022 - All rights reserved.**

The content contained within this book may not be reproduced, duplicated or transmitted without direct written permission from the author or the publisher.

Under no circumstances will any blame or legal responsibility be held against the publisher, or author, for any damages, reparation, or monetary loss due to the information contained within this book. Either directly or indirectly. You are responsible for your own choices, actions, and results.

Legal Notice:

This book is copyright protected. This book is only for personal use. You cannot amend, distribute, sell, use, quote or paraphrase any part, or the content within this book, without the consent of the author or publisher.

Disclaimer Notice:

Please note the information contained within this document is for educational and entertainment purposes only. All effort has been executed to present accurate, up to date, and reliable, complete information. No warranties of any kind are declared or implied. Readers acknowledge that the author is not engaging in the rendering of legal, financial, medical or professional advice. The content within this book has been derived from various sources. Please consult a licensed professional before attempting any techniques outlined in this book.

By reading this document, the reader agrees that under no circumstances is the author responsible for any losses, direct or indirect, which are incurred as a result of the use of the information contained within this document, including, but not limited to, — errors, omissions, or inaccuracies.

CONTENTS

Introduction — 9

1. PRINCIPLES OF LANDSCAPING — 17
   The Different Elements of Landscaping — 18
   Do It Yourself or Hire a Professional? — 19
   Getting Started on your Landscaping Project — 20
   Managing Your Time for Landscaping — 21
   Identifying your Theme and Style — 23
   The Cost of Landscaping — 25
   The Benefits of Doing Your Own Landscaping — 27
   The Main Elements of Landscaping — 29
   The Principles of Landscape Design — 32

2. DESIGNING FOR YOUR NEEDS — 39
   The First Steps in Your Landscaping Process — 40
   Evaluating Your Outdoor Area — 43
   Researching Your Plants — 47
   Designing Your Landscape — 48
   Including Different Elements in Your Design — 50
   Designing for Privacy — 53
   Designing for Other Functions — 57
   Tips to Get You Started — 58

3. PREPARING YOUR SITE — 61
   When to Begin — 62
   Different Jobs for Different Seasons — 63
   Preparing Your Yard — 67

Revisit Your Plan	70
Preparing Your Landscaping Beds	71
4. INCORPORATING HARDSCAPE ELEMENTS	77
5. ALL ABOUT PLANTS	95
Things to Consider when Choosing Your Plants	113
Your Climate and Your Garden	114
6. OVERCOMING CHALLENGES	117
Drainage Issues	119
Hot Climate Issues	122
Eyesores and Other Issues	125
Assessing Your Progress	127
7. PROJECTS TO GET YOU STARTED	129
How to Build a Flower Bed	130
How to Build a Raised Flower Bed	131
How to Build a Simple Wood-Burning Fire Pit	132
How to Build a Simple Patio	133
How to Edge a Garden Bed with Bricks, Pavers, or Stones	135
How to Install a Walkway	136
How to Create a Pond	138
Looking Ahead	140
Conclusion: Continue Your Landscaping Journey	147
Sources	155

A FREE GIFT FOR OUR READERS

9 awful mistakes that all gardeners make. Break bad habits and find the solutions to your problems.

JOIN OUR GROUP

Connect with over 600 like-minded individuals. Share photos, discuss projects and discover the secret recipe to keeping your garden in tip-top shape!

Scan the QR code below to join!

INTRODUCTION

Your outdoor space is an essential part of your home. It's where you spend time with your family, bask in the fresh air, and make lasting memories that stay with you for the rest of your life. To create a useful and appealing outdoor space, you have to ensure that it aligns with your needs. When I first began my landscaping journey, I was overwhelmed by the sheer amount of possibilities that were at my disposal. I was unsure of whether I should hire a company to bring my landscaping dreams to life or whether I should attempt to do it all myself. Once I ran the numbers, it was far too expensive to go the professional route, and that's why I ended up conducting an extensive amount of research to learn the ins and outs of the landscaping process. Now that I have four years of experience under my belt, I'm here to share with you all of the fundamentals of landscaping design so you can excel at your own journey.

I wanted a space that felt just as much like home as the interior of my house. I hoped for a beautiful, comfortable space where I could entertain my friends and family, as well as grow vegetables to enrich my health. I planned ahead, took my time with every tedious task until it became easier, and learned a great deal about what to avoid. The mistakes I made along the way served as great lessons for what I shouldn't do in the future, and they have truly helped me maintain my space without feeling overwhelmed. No matter how big or small your current space may be, it still packs a lot of potential. I've learned to make the best use of small spaces, and that has helped me organize my outdoor space effectively so that I can best enjoy it.

A few simple design tricks and some organization skills can transform a space that once felt cluttered or overwhelming, making it a place you want to spend time. Now that you're looking for a fresh start for your outdoor space, it's a good time to make a list of all your needs and wants. Stick to realistic goals while you begin the planning process of your landscape design. While we may all sometimes wish we had a bit more space to include another architectural element or a water feature, we sometimes have to make sacrifices for the good of the space. The last thing you want is to make your outdoor area feel even more unusable than it already is. I will walk you through all of the steps and techniques to improve your landscape while learning all the necessary skills to ensure it remains a beautiful space for you to enjoy.

You may be asking yourself, "how do I know which plants to go with? How do I know which elements will work for my space the best?" By the time you've made it halfway through, you'll feel confident in your landscaping abilities, and inspired to make your outdoor space an absolute dream.

The best way to approach landscape design is to think of it like you would interior design. Think about the processes you used to purchase the furniture for your home, or how you chose the right paint colors to complement your space. The same rules apply to designing your landscape to fit your desired theme while maintaining its functionality.

Your landscape design needs to align with your desires, but it also needs to take into consideration where you're located, and how your weather patterns could affect your space. If you live in warm, humid climates and experience quite a great deal of rain, you'll base a lot of your design decisions around that so that you can maximize the usage of your space. However, if you live in a climate that goes through a variety of seasonal changes, especially with regard to snow, you'll choose your design plans much more carefully so that you don't ruin all of your hard work. Think about all of the activities you'd like to do in your outdoor space, whether that'd be entertaining, gardening, including play areas for your children, or anything else that comes to mind. Take some time out of your day to sit outside, enjoy some fresh air, and begin visualizing what you'd like your outdoor area to look like.

While there are abundant possibilities for your space, it will take time to choose the right ones. You'll weigh all the options, plan ahead, make sketches to avoid locking yourself into decisions that are difficult to change, and conduct your landscape design step by step at your own pace. It's preferable to take your landscaping process slowly, building on it effectively over time, instead of trying to get everything done at once. That will make your DIY job look professional. This book will provide you with everything you need to know to get started on your landscaping project.

Although you will make mistakes along the way, these shouldn't deter you from your goal. Think of each one as a lesson; you're probably not going to make the same mistake twice, and each mistake will lead you closer to the right choice.

> *"If you've never experienced the joy of accomplishing more than you can imagine, plant a garden."*
>
> — ROBERT BRAULT

Your landscape design process will be a transformative, exciting experience. A lot of people get discouraged when it comes to big projects like landscaping because they doubt their own abilities. Although you've probably never taken on a project like this, you can do this. I started my landscaping design journey wondering if I could really turn my outdoor space into something extraordinary, and I managed to do just that. The key to success here, like with anything else, is consistency.

Once you've established a solid plan of action and laid the foundation for your design, everything else will fall into place. The best part about doing your own landscaping is that you have full creative control, and you're able to work around your own schedule. You'll be able to do much more than you think once you've learned all of the tips and techniques that will guide your process. Even though mistakes will be made, that doesn't mean that you should give up and dish out hundreds of dollars on a professional company just yet.

Give yourself a genuine chance to succeed, and you'll start to see incredible things happen.

One of the biggest mistakes you can make with your landscape design process is to skip the planning and get straight to work. People who do this end up with an outdoor space they hate, feeling like they wasted a lot of time and money. You're going to run into quite a few obstacles if you don't plan properly, and throughout this book, you'll learn how to do that effectively.

Another common mistake is neglecting to plan for the long term. Your flower choices may look good right now, but are they going to hold up throughout the year? The same goes for any architectural elements that you include, which are much harder to move around. If you're not going to like how it looks through the majority of your climate's seasonal changes, it may be best to skip it. Your area may feel drab in the winter, but you can at least make sure you like your outdoor spaces as much as possible even on gray days, and that you continue to love them during the more colorful times of the year.

If you plan for long-term success, you won't overwhelm yourself with excessive upkeep to keep your outdoor space flourishing. I had to dial back a lot of the design choices I had made initially because they didn't align with what I wanted to achieve, and it only made things feel more unusable than before. With the information you'll find in later chapters, you'll be well on your way to designing and creating an outdoor space that will enrich your entire life.

The first thing you need to do as you begin planning your landscape is to set a budget. How much are you willing to spend? Break it down into smaller, more manageable increments and work on it over time instead of dishing out the cash all at once. This way you will be able to work comfortably without feeling overwhelmed by the thought that you might be wasting your time and money. For example, I invested in the right tools, which is a significant up-front expense, but saves both time and money later. Then I learned everything I could about landscaping, so that I understood my limits within the "do-it-yourself" approach.

Keep your vision simple and clean. Everyone's idea of a perfect outdoor space is going to look and feel different. Even as you take the time out of your day to research and find reference pictures to help get a better sense of what you like, don't try to include too many elements that will only act as distractions in your space. You don't want outdoor clutter any more than you want indoor clutter. Everything you add should serve a purpose. Armed with that mindset, you'll be able to avoid having to add and remove too many items because they don't seem to fit over time.

Finally, landscaping and gardening are both skills that enhance your everyday life. They allow you to focus your attention on something other than your never-ending responsibilities. Allow yourself to enjoy every step of the process, and bask in the act of getting outdoors to make your outdoor area a beautiful and useful space.

Now that you've learned a little bit about what it's going to take to transform your landscape into one you will love, it's time you learned more about the actual process of landscaping.

1

PRINCIPLES OF LANDSCAPING

Landscaping refers to making improvements on a property's grounds in a practical or aesthetic way. This includes the planning, laying out, and construction of gardens that enhance the appearance and usability of an outdoor space.

Different people have different reasons for landscaping their property, depending largely on their goals and desires for their outdoor space. Some people want to put the space to some practical use, rather than having it sit empty and unproductive. Others want their outdoor space to be a welcoming place to entertain friends and family. No matter what the individual's goals, landscaping is the path to making them happen.

THE DIFFERENT ELEMENTS OF LANDSCAPING

Your outdoor space is just as important to your property as the interior of your home, and yet so many people neglect it. When I first moved into my home, taking care of my outdoor space was the last thing on my mind. But I was missing out on the ability to enjoy the space, an area I paid for along with the rest of my home, and I knew that had to change. You might be ready to learn more as well, to put effort into your outdoor space, and create something incredible. The first step to doing that is to increase your knowledge of the ups and downs of landscaping.

One of the most important elements of landscaping, and often one of the most intimidating, is plants. Plants can be decorative, edible, or just pretty, and can add visual interest as well as functionality to your space. Another important facet is terrain, which refers to the shape of the land. This can be modified or changed altogether through grading, backfilling, mounding, terracing, and more. In addition to plants and terrain, there are structures you can incorporate to enhance your outdoor space such as fences, patio covers, walls, decks, and planters. It will take time, research, and planning to decide which of these elements, and in what combination, best fits your outdoor space and your goals for it.

The thought of having to tackle every category on my own terrified me at first, especially because I didn't have the skill set necessary to pull it off. However, I started small with tasks that felt the least intimidating, slowly moving into tasks that were more challenging over time. This allowed me to learn as I progressed, without getting frustrated or discouraged because I had taken on too much all at once. Remember, you're not going to landscape your entire outdoor space in one go. Your goal is to encourage the slow growth of your yard at a pace that is manageable to you.

DO IT YOURSELF OR HIRE A PROFESSIONAL?

If you are reading this book, you are at least considering doing your landscaping by yourself, rather than hiring professionals. While it may be necessary to hire someone for the more dangerous or difficult sections of your landscape design, such as electrical or architectural features, it's very possible to do the rest of the project on your own.

While the DIY way may seem intimidating, it truly is an easy and affordable way to get the look you want without having to put too much money down. Projects such as patios, fences, or gardening are all tasks that you can certainly do on your own, and with a little practice, the skills involved will come easier to you. The key here is not to take on too much when you first begin your landscaping design project, because that's how a lot of people end up giving up entirely. If you take it in small steps, you will have full creative control over how the finished project looks, and the satisfaction of knowing you did it with your own two hands.

GETTING STARTED ON YOUR LANDSCAPING PROJECT

To begin with, focus on your needs and wants for your outdoor space. As was mentioned before, the research and planning stage is absolutely necessary, so don't skip it! Take the time to enjoy it, build up the anticipation that will inspire you to get started, and begin analyzing your skill set. Do some research on the areas in which you feel the most uncomfortable tackling so that you can read up on what not to do as well as how to get the job done effectively. Peruse different articles and blog posts on anything specific that you want to accomplish for your landscape so that you'll have a better idea of how to get the look you want.

When you're making a list of all the tasks you'll have to tackle during your landscape transformation, outline the more manageable tasks to begin with. This will keep you from getting overwhelmed, and it will inspire you to keep going. While you might run into some obstacles, you'll be learning a great deal about how to landscape effectively, and those small, early successes will keep you going until you have the outdoor space you've always dreamed of.

MANAGING YOUR TIME FOR LANDSCAPING

Your greatest asset with regard to your landscape design process is your time. Whether you're trying to fit the work into your already busy schedule or you're hoping to take advantage of the free time you have to improve your outdoor space, the time you invest is essential. You have to decide what works best for you, and how that time is going to play a role in the growth you're aiming for. No one expects you to have your landscape finished in a few days or even weeks. Good work takes time to accomplish, and acknowledging that will help you work through some of the most difficult times in your landscaping journey.

If you don't have time on your hands, you can always look into outsourcing the work so that you can stick within your budget, but also guarantee that work is being done. Here are some questions to ask during the planning process so that you can effectively tackle the start of your project:

1. How much am I willing to spend to get this done?
2. Am I capable of handling a majority of the tasks, or learning to handle them, or should I look into hiring a company?
3. How much help would I need to do it myself?
4. How much time can I dedicate to this project every week?
5. What do I want to get out of this landscaping project?

Struggling to manage your time? Constantly falling short of your goals? Looking for someone to hold you accountable? Then look no further. Join our fantastically fun Facebook community! Interact with others, Share photos and find friends!

Scan any one of the QR codes below to get started today!

IDENTIFYING YOUR THEME AND STYLE

Once you have an idea of how you're going to start, consider what your landscape style is. Different themes and expressions have different requirements, and your first step in deciding what you like is to find some inspiration. Remember, it's important to be realistic when you're looking for reference pictures because it's easy to get carried away with elements that simply won't work for your outdoor space. You have to work with what you have, and acknowledge the small tweaks you can make at the very start that could very well make a significant difference. The easiest way I've found to outline the theme I went with was to focus on the three categories I wanted to include, which were:

entertaining, vegetable gardening, and flower gardening.

This helped me decide on a minimal yet beautiful outdoor space that remains organized to this day. I found reference pictures like the ones below that helped me visualize these elements in my own space as well as ensure that every attribute chosen complemented each other.

As you note the more manageable tasks in your planning process, be sure to also note the ones where you might need a bit more support to accomplish. Complicated beds and hardscaping elements may require professionals to be done effectively. You get to decide how much or how little of these elements you'd like to incorporate into your space depending on your budget, time, and overall theme of your outdoor area. Don't rush into any decisions that are going to be difficult to change in the future. Take the process one step at a time, and you'll be well on your way to designing a landscape that encompasses all of your needs.

THE COST OF LANDSCAPING

A landscaping job can cost anywhere from $5,000 to over $100,000 depending on what you're trying to accomplish as well as how much space you actually have to work with. When you're deciding on a budget and the improvements you're going to make to your outdoor space, remember that these changes are going to add value to your home. If you were to ever sell your home in the future, having a beautiful outdoor space will increase the price of your property, and it act as a great selling point. A general rule of thumb is to spend 10% of your home's value on landscaping. For example, if your home is $300,000 then you'd be looking to spend $30,000 on landscaping. However, landscaping may cost even more than this and that depends solely on your goals.

These figures might be scaring you, and you may be shaking your head thinking, "There's no way I can swing that kind of money right now." The key is to not spend it all in one go. You don't have to come up with a ridiculous figure and dish it all out at once. Start with one that you're comfortable spending, and if that still seems too big, break it down into smaller increments that will be more manageable for you as a result.

Remember, you can take as long as you need to get your outdoor space looking the way you'd like it to. You can make small changes over a long period of time if that's what you're most comfortable with. You're the homeowner, and in this case, the landscaper, so you get to make all the rules. If you're still struggling with your budget, you can speak to a landscape designer to have them break down the cost and create an overall plan for you to follow. This will help you to evaluate what you can do on your own, and what you may need professional support to accomplish correctly.

THE BENEFITS OF DOING YOUR OWN LANDSCAPING

There are so many benefits to landscaping that once you've created a budget and begun the process itself, you'll be able to see. Here are a few that made the decision to landscape my outdoor area much easier:

Property Value

Landscaping can add as much as 15% extra value to your property's value. This will increase your chances of having your property sell for more should you decide to list it in the future.

Creative Control

Having creative control over your outdoor space allows you to make changes as you go and ensures that you love every single element that you add into your space. You'll design your landscape based solely on your needs and preferences, and if your outdoor space currently isn't a perfect fit for you or your family, you get to change that. A family that isn't interested in gardening won't benefit from a yard that requires a lot of maintenance just as a family who doesn't cook often may not want an outdoor kitchen. You can add whatever you see fit to get the most out of your outdoor space.

Health Benefits

There are many health benefits to engaging in your landscaping process. While you work on the setup of your outdoor space, you're breathing in fresh air, and getting a considerable amount of Vitamin D from the sun, which is crucial to your health. Gardening has also been shown to have a positive impact on how you feel, and it's a good way to get movement in during the day if you've been looking to incorporate more exercise into your daily routine. If you opt to grow vegetables or fruits in your outdoor space, you can enjoy healthy meals regularly every time you harvest fresh produce.

Entertaining

Your outdoor space is great for spending time with your friends and family. Some of the best memories are made while soaking up the fresh air and sharing stories with the ones you love. Creating an inviting environment starts with a clean, relaxing patio. You may also want to add an outdoor kitchen or elements that will allow you to throw the best barbecues or brunches. The opportunities are endless when it comes to using your outdoor area for entertaining, and deciding what best suits your family will make the space truly feel like home.

THE MAIN ELEMENTS OF LANDSCAPING

Now that you know all the benefits of working on your landscape design, it's time to get into the fundamentals that will make the process itself easier on you. Here are the main elements of landscaping that you need to be aware of:

Form

Form refers to the structure of your elements as well as how it performs in your outdoor space. For example, the form of a plant refers to its shape and the structure of its branching pattern. Trees come in many shapes and range structurally from stiff and upright like poplar trees to drooping like weeping willows. You also need to consider the form of individual components, as well as the form that groups of them make when combined. Think about the size of the plants you're adding, along with the size and shape of the leaves to analyze their textures. This can have a significant impact on the way your garden spaces or other plant-heavy areas of your landscape look.

Texture

Texture refers to the visual and tactile surface of your elements as well as their quality. Mixing both plant textures and architectural textures will create a visually interesting space, keeping it pleasing to the eye. A good landscape designer will often mix textures to add variety and create zones throughout the landscape so it doesn't feel repetitive or overcrowded.

Line

Lines are used to give an illusion of depth and distance, and draw the eye in a particular direction or movement. Perspective can be influenced by the arrangement of plants or other elements as well as their borders. This creates a sense of flow throughout the space, allowing it to feel cohesive and complete. One tip is to use vertical lines to pull the view upwards, making the space feel larger. Trees or arbors can add vertical lines in your outdoor space. Horizontal lines can also make the space feel larger by pulling the view along the ground. This is done through elements such as garden walls, walkways, or small hedges. Choosing the right elements to create flow is integral to its overall functionality.

Color

Color is used to give your landscape dimension and accentuate certain areas. Color can be added with both plant and architectural elements. The ones you choose can really transform your space and create certain feelings. Blues and greens create perspective because they feel like they're moving away when you look at them. Warm colors have the opposite effect, making objects appear closer as a result. Colors can be used in a variety of ways depending on your landscaping goals, including creating different moods, attracting wildlife, drawing attention to important features, or providing seasonal variety.

Scale

The scale of an element refers to its size in relation to other things in your landscape. Choosing elements of the right scale or complementary scales will help you to create visual appeal without becoming too distracting or overwhelming. Play around with different sizes of elements to determine which works best for your space. It's important to acknowledge the overall size of your landscape to ensure that no element you choose disrupts the flow of your outdoor area. When arranging objects of different scales, one technique is to use odd numbers of certain elements to create a sense of liveliness or energy, or even numbers to convey stability and strength. Even numbers can be alternated with odd numbers to convey both unity and vibrancy in your design.

There are endless opportunities for combining these elements of landscape design to create an unforgettable space. Every element you include should be adding something positive to your space, and should combine with all the other elements to create an overall pleasing aesthetic.

THE PRINCIPLES OF LANDSCAPE DESIGN

Knowing the above elements of landscape design is an important first step, and will help you begin considering how to achieve your ideas concerning height, depth, space, and mood. But there is more to know if you hope to arrange all these elements in an effective layout that accomplishes your vision. These principles of landscape design will help you avoid clutter, chaos, and sloppiness, and will help you choose your items and placements so that your vision is realized.

Proportion

Proportion refers to the balance of the elements within the space. With proportionality, elements complement each other in terms of the space they take up, the attention they demand, and the flow of the eye across the big picture. A garden or landscape that is out of proportion has a lack of transition. Elements appear abruptly placed, and the viewer may be confused why they are positioned the way they are. Different elements may have different inherent proportions, especially hardscapes (architectural elements such as fences or walkways) and softscapes (plants), which tend to stand out apart from other parts of the landscape disproportionately. The overall goal is for their proportions to create an effective balance throughout your design.

Order/Balance

An orderly or balanced space realizes the concept of proportionality in the way that elements are spaced within the landscape. Proportionality has to do with how strongly each elements draws the viewer's attention, and balance has to do with placing each element so that together they create visual interest, and no piece overwhelms the sense of the whole. Depending on your tastes, you may choose a symmetrical or asymmetrical balance in your outdoor area. In symmetrical balance, both sides of your landscape are identical and they utilize the same elements to give a unified effect. However, in asymmetrical balance, the composition uses different elements with similar visual weight that complement each other. Symmetrical balance tends to feel more secure, more settled, and more predictable-- qualities that make people feel safe and comforted. Asymmetrical balance tends to be more energetic, more unique, and offer more opportunities to showcase someone's personality or creative touch. Symmetrical tends to be more classically beautiful, while asymmetrical is often considered more fun and artistic. Of course, how you choose to balance your elements will depend heavily on the lay of the land and buildings as well as your personal expression.

Repetition/Rhythm

The idea behind repetition and rhythm in your landscape is to create familiar patterns and predictable sequences. This familiarity helps to create balance between your elements and it guarantees that your space benefits from a symmetrical perspective. When you have design elements or other features repeat throughout your landscape it creates a sense of continuity. The repetition alone can help draw the eye in and guide it throughout the entire space. Having too many unrelated items can make your design feel cluttered or unplanned. However, overusing elements can make your design feel very overwhelming, so it's important to use repetition to your advantage rather than allowing it to further clutter your space. Choose elements that work well in repetitive patterns and are on a relatively smaller scale to avoid creating a space that feels too messy.

Unity

Unity means that everything is connected and works together to create a whole. It is achieved by the careful use of the principles of balance and proportionality, and is the whole, or big-picture, result of careful choices made in each of these areas. Thoughtful placement of elements such as landscape plants in relation to their form and size helps to create a unified feel. This idea works with any element that you add into your space, and it will help you reach the goal of creating an overall theme in your outdoor area that sparks joy as well as promotes visual interest.

Focalization

Focalization means to create a focus of attention, or focal point. This can be a center around which all the other elements are organized, or it can be a splash of size or color that breaks up a visual line. The eye is immediately drawn to the focal points, and they are the strongest elements in your space. They're usually the ones that spark the most interest and conversation, and they serve different purposes throughout your outdoor space. For example, when you think of your home's focal point, it's usually the front door. The eye is always immediately drawn to the front door whenever you step onto someone's front porch. Therefore, the focal point of a landscape usually enhances the center itself or the entrance of your outdoor space. You can include as many focal points as your outdoor space needs, but too many can easily become overwhelming to the eye. Think of them as centerpieces that create balance in your landscape design.

Color Theory

Color theory is a principle that will help you properly organize different elements according to their colors so that they're either repetitive or complementary. The spectrum of color is divided into four categories:

- Primary colors: reds, yellows, and blues
- Secondary colors: greens, purples, and oranges
- Tertiary colors: blends of primary and secondary colors which create combinations like yellow-green, blue-green, or red-orange
- Natural colors: whites, grays, and silver

When you combine colors together, you can use the different facets of the spectrum to inspire a specific look for your landscape. Each decision that you make will produce a different effect. Blue, purple, and green are considered cool colors. They tend to have a calming or relaxing effect. Colors like red, yellow, or orange are considered warm colors and they excite as well as quickly draw the eye. Warm and cool colors can be manipulated to create different moods throughout your space, and they're good tools for sectioning different areas of your landscape into zones.

For example, combining warm and cool colors can change the perception of depth. Warm colors like red can make overly large spaces seem smaller and more intimate. The warm colors appear to come forward in the landscape and seem closer than they are in reality. Changing the perspective of your landscape is the quickest and most effective way to create visual interest without including too many distractions.

2

DESIGNING FOR YOUR NEEDS

What do you want to accomplish with your landscape design? Maybe you've been underutilizing your outdoor space, telling yourself that you'll find the budget and the time necessary to make use of it, but you never do. You dream of having the perfect outdoor area to entertain, enjoy time with your family, and make incredible memories.

What's stopping you? Your outdoor area is an extension of your home, and it's land that was factored into its price. While your outdoor space may not currently be the best fit for you and your family, designing it to fit your needs will genuinely change your life.

We often spend so much time inside, tending to responsibilities around the house or with our families, that we never give much thought to what's going on outside our back doors. We see the barren land or the single lawn chair, wishing we had somewhere to get some fresh air or grow our own vegetables, but it all just seems too difficult to accomplish. I used to think this way too, believing that it would take me ages to develop the landscape of my dreams, but it didn't. Every change I made was exciting, every new idea I learned made me want to improve, and my skills as a landscaper have grown exponentially over the past few years.

You don't have to start out with an enormous amount of landscaping knowledge to succeed in making your outdoor space fit your current lifestyle. You just need to be willing to learn.

THE FIRST STEPS IN YOUR LANDSCAPING PROCESS

You've got all the principles down, understand how the elements work, and you've begun looking for reference pictures to help you visualize what you want your own outdoor space to be, so now it's time to talk about your first steps. You probably already have an idea of what your tastes are and what designs appeal to you the most, and now your task is to combine those creative ideas with your goals for your space's functionality.

What are your main landscaping goals? Think about all the factors that are going to influence your decisions, such as:

- Your children
- Sustainability
- Entertaining
- Increasing real estate value
- Relaxation
- Privacy

Begin by making a list of the different elements that are absolute requirements in your space, and include them in your final landscape design plan. This plan doesn't have to have a specific technique or method to be effective. It's about knowing what your limits and capabilities are, as well as putting those to the test as you embark on your landscaping journey. Pull out a piece of blank paper and start making rough sketches of what you'd like your landscape to look like. There are no wrong additions. You get to decide what's going to look good in your space and what elements are going to work for you and your family.

When I first started collecting my own landscaping ideas, I made a folder on my computer as well as a physical binder I kept on hand to collect any magazine clippings or articles I came across. I wasn't just looking for beautifully shot photographs, but also clear methods that seemed easy enough to tackle on my own. I learned a lot from making many mistakes when I first started landscaping on my own, and I will tell you that if something feels too challenging even after you've learned all you can about it, don't be afraid to hire out for those tasks. There were architectural and electrical details that I tried adding on my own which quickly became too difficult. When tasks like these are not completed correctly they can be dangerous. Include the tasks that you'd consider hiring out for in your overall plan. This will help you to avoid any large problems that are going to cost more money to fix than it would to hire the right people for the job. One thing that gave me a lot of insight while creating my landscaping plan was to consult gardening magazines and websites. I carefully combed through a lot of information, deciding what I needed for my space, and what I could omit entirely.

This may seem like an overwhelming process at first, but you're allowed to enjoy it. Don't allow it to stress you to the point where you're considering giving up altogether. Remember, no matter how big of a task you set out to accomplish, it can always be broken down into smaller, more manageable increments. Once I gave into the excitement, versus spending all my time worrying that I was going to do something wrong, the mistakes didn't feel so large anymore. I was able to work around them, fix any problems I came across, and continue building the landscape of my dreams. Creating a solid plan will take time, but it will become the guide that you will reference at every step of your process to make your landscape design as painless as possible.

EVALUATING YOUR OUTDOOR AREA

Now that you've begun collecting information and inspiration, it's time to study your outdoor area. Start by observing your landscape at different times during the day so you can discern which areas receive more sunlight than others, how it appears in the morning versus the evening, and what the different conditions are that may affect your landscape care. If you live in a place that is consistently hot or receives a lot of rain, you'll probably choose elements that can withstand these conditions, and the same goes for seasonal changes such as snow. Your landscape has to have enough flexibility built in to allow it to adapt to changes, especially if it's going to bounce back during the peak times of the year. Take note of how long the sun is out and what your landscape looks like during hectic weather conditions such as torrential rain-- observing how your space reacts in a few intense storms will give you a good idea of what you'll need for speedy cleanup once the weather clears.

Many people who begin landscaping for themselves are afraid of the maintenance because they add too many elements that require a hefty amount of upkeep. Choose your elements and arrange them in a way so that the maintenance fits your lifestyle. If you do not want to include garden elements where you'll be harvesting your own vegetables, you can leave them out. If you're not going to be entertaining much, you can arrange your patio space for other activities. The opportunities are truly endless when you're designing your landscape to fit your needs. Remember, you're trying to increase the usability of your outdoor space, as well as turning it into something you and your family enjoy.

One thing I noticed upon studying my own landscape was that morning sunshine is gentler on plants because the temperatures are lower. Acknowledge the times of day where the sunlight is harsher on your plants, and this will help you tend to them once you begin to work on your garden space. Learning to take care of your elements and your overall landscape is part of the job when it comes to creating as well as basking in the joy of having it. It doesn't have to be a difficult or tedious task. While you'll want to keep maintenance as low as possible, you have to decide what elements best suit your space, and how much time you're willing to invest in order to take care of them.

As you start to lay out your plan of action, measure your outdoor space and incorporate those figures into any sketches you have. This will help tremendously when you're choosing elements because you won't pick anything that's disproportionate or would instantly overwhelm your space. It will be much easier to pick the elements that work when you have a reference in mind to ensure all sizes are complementary and everything is at the appropriate scale.

If planning solely on paper doesn't help you to properly visualize how elements may look in your space, you may opt for using hoses or rope to make imaginary boundaries for plant beds. You can also use larger miscellaneous items to represent larger plants like shrubs and trees. Much of what you're going to be planting will take time to fully grow and blossom, so make sure to allow for changes in size when spacing larger elements. Your landscape may not appear fully finished until that happens, but don't let this take away from your planning process. When I did this in my own backyard, I took photos of the entire landscape once I'd laid out where I wanted the different elements to go. In an editing software, I created a mock-up of what it would look like utilizing fully grown gardening pictures that I had saved for reference. This was another great way to help me visualize how it could turn out once everything was finally laid down, and it helped me identify the small changes I wanted to make immediately.

Laying out your placeholder items will take trial and error. You're going to move things around often as well as change the way your visuals look over time. You don't have to have everything figured out at the start of your process, and even when you've already begun, you may find yourself wanting to change things around. That is completely okay because at the end of the day, you're creating a space that you love. You shouldn't have to live with landscape design decisions you're unhappy with, but to avoid making too many of these mistakes at the start, planning is truly crucial.

RESEARCHING YOUR PLANTS

When it comes to the plants for your outdoor space, consider the ones you love as well as the ones that are fitting for your climate. This will be discussed in detail in a later chapter, but for now try to gather as much information as possible, finding out what plants, textures, colors, and overall feel express your individual style. Begin researching what plants would work best in your outdoor space, considering the size as well as the upkeep that they'll need to flourish.

There are many ways to research plants to get a feel for how they might contribute to your landscape. Gardening and landscaping websites have excellent ideas for combining elements in different climates and different kinds of outdoor spaces. Plant catalogues and home and garden magazines feature different themes each month or each season so you can get ideas to apply to your own space. Perhaps the best way to learn about plants is to go to a greenhouse or nursery and see them in person. This way you can experience their scent and texture as well as their color, or put them physically side by side to see how they complement each other, and get a sense of how they will enhance the beauty of your space.

You don't have to commit to any specific plants yet, but having a sense of what you like will give you peace of mind, inspiration, and creative ideas as you begin to lay the groundwork for your landscape.

DESIGNING YOUR LANDSCAPE

Designing your landscape can be done with any method you're most comfortable with. If you're not comfortable with laying out your designs on a piece of paper, you can take it to the computer to lay out a mock-up like I did, or you can stick to solely marking off your outdoor area with placeholder items. I found that utilizing both paper planning and computer programs worked the best for me because it gave me more options for visualizing my finished landscape. Keep in mind that you need to be adding the mature versions of your plants to your design, because each plant looks different at various stages of its growth and that can affect the overall look of your space.

The first question to ask as you begin your design is what style appeals to you. Some people appreciate a lush, full landscape, with one zone flowing into the other across the entire space. Others prefer a minimalistic or subtle look, with clean lines and a few well-chosen focal points. Deciding on a style will help you appropriately lay out your landscape without trying to add too many elements which would distract from both its appeal as well as its functionality. Visualizing the overall feel is one of the most important initial steps,but it's key to ensuring your landscape turns out the way you hope.

When you research different landscape styles, notice which elements are the most prevalent in each one. While you design your landscape, you'll also want to think about the amount of maintenance you're willing to do to keep your outdoor area flourishing. The last thing you want is to put hours, days, even weeks of work into your space only to let it become an overgrown mess due to the lack of upkeep. Having an idea of how often you'd be actively working on your outdoor space, tending to your plants, fixing any broken items or features, will allow you to design it so those tasks do not become tedious. When I finally designed the landscape of my dreams, I found that I wasn't dreading the upkeep at all because I made it fit my own schedule.

Another thing to think about is whether you're planning to stay in your home forever or if you plan to list it for sale a few years down the road. Once you decide on this, you'll have a clearer picture of your priorities, and that can also help you pinpoint the style that's going to work the best for your outdoor space. A property that's going to be sold in the near future needs more "curb appeal" than a house you plan to stay in long-term because you're going to be trying to capture the interest of potential buyers.

INCLUDING DIFFERENT ELEMENTS IN YOUR DESIGN

Up to this point, you've considered your personal style, the commitment you're willing to make to upkeep, and the longevity your landscaping vision requires. The next step to designing this vision is to consider different landscaping features that may be integral to your design choices. They include:

- Planting beds
- Lawns
- Shrubs
- Flowering trees
- Driveways
- Walkways
- Fences
- Fountains
- Water gardens

There are many more elements that you can choose from, but these are a good place to start when it comes to designing an appealing landscape. You get to decide how best to balance your landscape's visual interest and its practicality, without overwhelming the space you already have. You may feel the urge to add as many elements as you can fit in your space, but sometimes leaving a bit of room throughout your elements will make the biggest difference. Your space should promote ease, relaxation, and enjoyment. Therefore, choose the elements that matter the most to you, and the ones that are going to make you happy once you see them in your space.

The elements listed above are just a few of the popular and common ones found on many people's properties. Your goal is to mix and match them to fit your personal style, but don't feel like you have to fit yourself into a box while doing so. Have fun with the elements you choose as you experiment with the best ways to arrange everything you've chosen.

Some styles of landscaping are better suited to some climates than others, and when you're choosing yours, consider what's native to your area, what will grow there, and how easily it will thrive. Here are a few examples:

- Xeriscape/Desert Landscape
- Tropical Landscape
- English Cottage Landscape

- Southwestern Landscape
- Minimalist Landscape
- Japanese Garden Landscape

DESIGNING FOR PRIVACY

Once you've decided on your stylistic choices or general look, include some landscaping design attributes that pertain to your privacy. Designing for privacy gives you some control over what your neighbors are able to see and allows you to be visible to your level of comfort. There are a number of different options when it comes to increasing the privacy around your outdoor space.

Hardscape vs Softscape Elements for Privacy

There are two easy-to-build hardscape methods that can serve your desire for privacy in your own space: fences and walls. They are considered "hardscape" because once they are placed, they become permanent features and do not change from season to season.

Fences are generally the go-to element for establishing a boundary between your space and someone else's-either the public spaces of the street or sidewalk, or the personal spaces belonging to neighbors. Within the fence is your own space. Most fences are built of hardwoods, which are more expensive than softwoods, but last longer and withstand the outdoor elements for much longer. Even though it's a bigger investment up front, a hardwood fence with worth the extra expense. Hardwoods often retain their finish and remain smooth and visually appealing for longer than softwoods as well. Whether hardwood or softwood, fences offer enough flexible choices in height, visibility, and color to be a perfect element in your overall design.

The other hardscape element that can provide privacy to your outdoor space is a wall. There are two main kinds of walls: masonry walls and living walls. Masonry walls are made of some kind of stone, and layered together with concrete or mortar in between layers to provide stability and a solid foundation for some element of your landscape. A masonry wall can be a few inches high and provide a border for a flowerbed, or it can be many feet high to provide a secure boundary to your property or some piece of it. Most walls are somewhere in between and provide reliable structure within the bounds of your outdoor space. Like fences, there is a great variety in the size, height, style, and color of a stone wall.

Walls and fences have a great advantage when used in landscaping. They are strong enough to enforce a boundary. They don't move. They do not decay, or if they do, it happens very slowly, over decades or even centuries. They are comprised of natural elements that complement the other landscaping choices. And of course, they are not see-through, which means that they will guard your privacy to the exact degree you want them to.

However, there are other ways to provide shelter and impede the view into your area from the outside. These are the "softscape" elements. They are organic elements such as trees, bushes, shrubs, grasses, plants, and flowers. A well-chosen living element can not only beautify the space, it can keep people from looking into and wandering into it if you don't want them to. It's not easy to sneak past a row of evergreen bushes, or to see past the flowering branches of a crabapple tree. Your security and privacy could be assured by something you originally chose for its beauty.

Both hardscape and softscape have advantages and disadvantages. A hardscape element is immediate; a fence or wall can be built within a few days, and then it is there for as long as you want it. Trees and bushes must be planted and tended and may take years to grow, especially to a size that will afford you some protection. While it's true that you can by fully grown trees, bushes, and shrubs, these are often prohibitively expensive, and most people choose to buy them as seeds or seedlings and grow them up within the space.

Hardscaping is easy to care for, as well. A wall doesn't need watering or trimming like a bush does. A fence won't die if you neglect it. However, it's the very aliveness of the softscape elements that appeal to some people. They like the sense that they are protecting their home and their privacy, but in a way that feels natural and nurturing.

While there are many options for hardscape in terms of the kind of wood or stone you choose, the creative possibilities for softscaping are almost endless. A fence or wall will always be exactly what you put there in the beginning, but a tree or shrub can come in infinite sizes, colors, and textures. It might give you flowers in the springtime and produce fruit for you in the fall. It might provide a home for songbirds or rustle in the breeze. While there is appeal to artistic stability of a fence or wall, only nature can provide the multisensory experience of a softscape.

Whichever option you choose to go with for your outdoor space, ensure that it fits the overall theme you envision. While privacy may be an important function for your landscaping, fencing and walls are elements that are seen from every angle of your outdoor area. Therefore, they should be visually appealing as well.

DESIGNING FOR OTHER FUNCTIONS

Although privacy is a significant function of landscaping, there are many other things your outdoor elements can do in addition to looking beautiful and turning away prying eyes. For example, strategically planted trees can reduce the heating or cooling needs of a home and drastically reduce the costs associated with them. Plants can reduce heat gain by keeping the sun from directly striking a building, and preventing reflected light from entering. Factoring these decisions into your landscaping design can help cut down your energy bills, and create more sustainable living for you and your family.

You can also create a habitat for wildlife by planting flowers that will attract pollinators like bees or butterflies. These are great additions to your outdoor area that can can bring joy while also doing great things for the environment. Other landscaping choices that can have a positive environmental impact include terracing to prevent erosion, composting to fertilize gardens and flowerbeds and to reduce landfill waste and chemical runoff into the soil, and the incorporation of solar or wind energy to reduce your home's consumption of fossil fuels.

TIPS TO GET YOU STARTED

As you consider the form, function, style, and feel of your developing landscape design, keep the following tips in mind. These will help you to keep focused, on budget, and excited about the work ahead of you.

Don't Be Impulsive

Use a thoughtful approach for both hardscaping and plants, rather than buying something on a whim that may not go with your overall design. Evaluate your choices based on budget to buy, install, and upkeep, as well as how much time you'd have to spend maintaining it. Once you've developed and created your vision, keep it in mind at all times.

Stick to Your Budget

After developing your plan, put real numbers to it and decide what you can and want to spend over the course of the landscaping project. Many landscaping projects span years or include gradual transitions from one design to another. Don't feel rushed to complete the project because taking your time will allow you to pay for things over time while still making progress.

Set a Time Budget

Think about how much time you'll have to dedicate to your projects once you get started. Will you be working on weekends or after work? By looking at the time requirements ahead of time you can avoid overcommitting to too many projects, or a project that is too large of a scale to be worth doing it by yourself. You may decide to forego the exotic rose bush--lovely as it is--and go instead with a serviceable evergreen or fern because they don't need as much attention. After all, the point of landscaping is to add quality to your life, not stress.

It's important to have a big-picture plan, but you don't have to have everything figured out before you start digging into the ground. Any mistakes you make can be fixed and any changes you see fit to make are worth it if they're going to help you enjoy your finished product more. And it's all too easy to tweak your design forever without ever feeling ready to get your hands dirty. But the point of all that designing is to create real change, and that's what you'll get started in the next chapter.

3

PREPARING YOUR SITE

The thought of cleaning up, organizing, and clearing out your site might feel overwhelming at this point. Some people never even begin the process, because they just don't know where or how to begin. When I first started my landscaping process, I was convinced that the preparation alone was going to be a hassle, and I was almost defeated before I even started. But that was before I did enough research to outline a plan that would work for me. The true key to any successful project is a clear, effective plan.

A lot of people think that landscaping and gardening must be difficult tasks because they involve so many steps and techniques, but that isn't the case. You can take things slowly, learn more as you go, and put what you've learned into practice. That is the best way to grow your landscaping knowledge and skills. With a timeline and design for your hardscaping and planting projects, you can take the steps to transform your entire yard.

WHEN TO BEGIN

Begin planning your landscaping process well in advance of the season in which you'd like to enjoy your outdoor space. For example, if you start a project mid-spring you probably won't have it finished by mid-summer, which is when you'd most likely want to use it. The ideal time to get landscaping work done is the fall, winter, or possibly early spring depending on the length of the project itself.

If your plan involves installing stone paving, walls, water features, or a fire pit you should consider completing these projects during the fall or winter. Structural work can take up a lot of time and space, making it so you can't use your yard during optimal weather if you try to do your construction then. It's a common misconception that these kinds of projects cannot be done during the winter months. Where materials like concrete may not be the best option to work on, due to cement needing the right conditions to properly cure, you can work on just about any other materials in the cold. If concrete isn't something that you're going to be including much of in your design, then feel free to get to work utilizing other materials while making the most of the time frame you have during seasons like fall or winter.

DIFFERENT JOBS FOR DIFFERENT SEASONS

Spring

Starting in the spring may seem like the best idea because it's finally getting warm outside, but it might actually set you back quite a bit. Landscaping projects can take months, especially if you only work on them on the weekends or evenings, and starting in the spring may mean that your yard is torn up or in transition all through the spring and summer, when you would most like to enjoy it. Spring is an ideal time to do smaller jobs that only take a few hours or a couple of days.

One of the challenges of working in the springtime that people often overlook is that while it is certainly wonderful to be enjoying the warmer weather and the resurgence of nature, spring can be volatile and unpredictable. The weather can fluctuate between cold snaps and heat waves, the rain can go on for weeks at a time, storms are violent and often accompanied by tornadoes, hail, and driving winds. All of these things can put tender new plants at risk, or damage trees that haven't had time to fully root. The result could easily be that you have to do all your work again once the weather calms down.

If spring is the only time you have to do concentrated work on your outdoor space, there are things you can do to get the most success from your work time.

- Check your temperatures. If early morning temperatures are expected to go below 45 degrees Fahrenheit, hold off on planting flowers or shrubs. The frost created on those cold mornings can kill your new plants.
- Check the soil. If the soil where you're hoping to plant is still frozen from the winter, or if it's saturated with water from spring rains, your

plants will not be able to firmly root. Soil should be firm but not hard, and moist but not wet.
- Focus on the best plants for the time of year. Dormant shrubs, small trees, and several vegetable crops do well when planted in the early spring. Cold-tolerant annual flowers, such as pansies, primroses, and violets, may also do well.

Summer

Summer seems like an ideal time to get some outdoor projects done, but it does have its drawbacks. For one thing, the physical labor that landscaping requires is difficult in extreme heat, and many parts of the world get very hot indeed. Plants will need extra water and additional care, putting you outside working even more. Excessive heat may cause your plants to struggle to thrive, especially while they are very young. In addition, summer is the time people try to relax a little, take vacations, and enjoy the outdoors, so consider whether you want to add a major landscaping project to your down time. Remember, landscaping is about adding quality to your life. Besides, if you have young plants and you go on vacation, they could be left without the care they need, and you could return to a sad and dying yard.

Fall

Early fall is generally the best time to get started on your projects. It's characterized by cooler temperatures and lower humidity, which will make the conditions much more comfortable for you as you work. Planting in the fall allows your trees, shrubs, and perennials to establish their root system so they're strong and ready to thrive in the springtime.

The more developed the root systems of your plants are, the better the plants will perform especially in the dramatic weather of spring and heat of summer. The early fall is also advantageous because you'll have favorable soil and moisture conditions along with the perfect temperatures to get the job done. In addition to the pleasant weather and extra rooting time, weeds don't grow as prolifically in the fall as in the spring and summer, so the hassle involved with weeding is minimized.

When I first started landscaping and gardening I was convinced that planting in the spring was the way to go, until I realized that my plants weren't thriving the way I wanted them to. That made me change my entire course of action. I began testing out each different season to see which one was the best fit for me, considering my schedule as well as what the outcome of my plants would be. Early fall was clearly the best choice for both my plants and me. It was a little harder for me to find free time to work, but since all the other elements were so perfect, it was worth the effort.

PREPARING YOUR YARD

Once you've decided which season to begin your landscaping and gardening projects in, it's time to figure out how to prepare your yard so you maximize your time while being as efficient as possible. First, make an inventory of your yard's permanent structures and map their placements so you'll know how best to work around them and with them. This may already have been part of your initial design for your space. If so, double check it to make sure it includes existing hardscape elements, underground or above ground utility lines, water or septic tanks, pipes, or other obstacles that could require you to take them into consideration. It's always best to consult your local building authority or utility companies before you begin any large digging projects so you can avoid any issues.

Next, remove any debris or dead plants from your yard. Debris could be rocks, leaves, sticks and branches, or trash that has blown in. If you have a compost pile or bin, add any dead plants or yard waste to it. This is a good time to weed-eat or edge your yard so you can see its true lines and angles without any overgrowth.

Now it's time to tackle the weeds in your garden. While it can be a tedious task, it must be done so that none of your new plants will be disrupted. Remove your weeds by pulling them out with your hands. If your yard itself is too large to do this efficiently, use a selective postemergence herbicide. Selective herbicides kill weeds while leaving your plants healthy and untouched. However, it's best not to rely solely on this to get rid of your weeds.

After weeding, prune and trim all of the plants that are going to remain part of your landscape. Remove all leaves and branches that are weak, diseased, or dying. You don't want these elements cluttering up your space, especially if you're going to be filling it with fresh, new plants. If you notice any diseased plants, remove them as soon as possible to prevent them from infecting existing plants or any new ones you add.

If you have any large hardscape elements that you need to remove, that can be done at this point. In some cases, this will require a professional, since not everyone is able to tear down a fence or a wall or chop down a tree on their own. Don't risk your safety if it's too big a job for you. It's worth the investment to get it done right.

The ground will need to be prepared if you plan to put down new sod. Remove the old grass and roots with a sod cutter. These will strip the lawn of grass and roots so that you're left with a blank slate of just soil. Till the yard to a depth of about eight inches and remove any rocks you find. Add your soil amendments, such as compost, then till again. After tilling is complete, smooth your yard using a yard roller, and you're ready to lay your sod.

An irrigation system requires advance work as well. You will need to determine if your home has enough water pressure to support outdoor irrigation by determining your water service flow rate. You do this by filling a five-gallon bucket with a hose and timing how long it takes, then dividing that figure by five. This will give you a gallons-per-minute (gpm) figure, which you will need in order to get a compatible irrigation system. Finally, map out exactly where your sprinklers will be installed, how much of an area of your landscape you want irrigated, and which sections will be covered in the sprinklers' radius.

REVISIT YOUR PLAN

It was hard for me to properly visualize the space when I was looking at all of the things that needed to be cleared out. Once I was finally looking at a clear yard, I put the pieces together quite easily. I was able to draw up new plans, decide where I wanted my hardscape elements to go, as well as lay out possible sections for my softscape elements. My entire plan began to change once I had a good look at how much space I genuinely had to work with.

Once you've taken the time to reprepare your yard, return to your original plan. If your plans no longer fit with the space you're currently looking at, it's time to revise them so that you won't have any wasted effort once you start. Take as much time with your second draft as you did with your first one, using the new awareness of your prepared yard to guide you.

PREPARING YOUR LANDSCAPING BEDS

Now that you've gotten your hands dirty cleaning up your yard, you should have a better sense of the size and scale of your space-and therefore what size and scale will work for your plant and flower beds. If you need to revise your original plan based on your new understanding of your space, this is one element that might require some attention. In your revised plan, you might decide that a different shape will look better, or that a differently sized version of the same shape will fit the space better. I always imagined that I would have enough space in my landscape for large square beds, but it wasn't until I started laying down my hardscape elements that I noticed there would be no way to fit them in without taking away from the work I'd already done. So, I took it back to the drawing board, scaling down the size of my landscape beds so that I could fit the ones I wanted into my space while keeping my theme consistent throughout.

Consider not just the size and scale of your beds, but how they work with the flow and lines of your design. If your landscape follows more informal patterns, your bed structure should reflect this. Rounded or curved shapes may fit nicely. However, if you've been working towards a formal landscape, then straight lines and angles would help you continue that clean, crisp look.

Knowing what effect you're going for will help you inspire the kind of continuity that will make your outdoor area the kind of place you want to spend your time.

I learned the hard way that trying to include too many elements just because I had the space was the wrong way to go. I strayed from my initial plan because I felt like I could figure it out as I went, but I quickly realized what a mistake that was. It took me a while to replant and reshape my beds to get them to look the way I wanted them to, and if I had planned better I would've been able to avoid the extra work.

When you're laying out your beds in your actual outdoor space, start by marking the edges of your bed area. Some people do this with an edging shovel, or you can use paint to make your edges clear. Dig into the ground about six inches deep around the border, cutting along that edge and angle the sides of the edges toward the bed to help keep your soil or mulch inside the boundary you are creating. Remove any current vegetation or any plant life that's still there because it could harm your fresh plants.

The next step is to grade the bed so that it doesn't collect water. Grading is the process of creating a smooth and slightly slanted surface, so that the water is directed one way and has no dips or valleys in which to collect. It is done through a combination of digging out higher places and filling in the dips until you get a smooth slope tilted the way you want it. It should be done well before you intend to actually plant in the bed, because the soil will settle or run off, and part of the grading process involves repeating it until it stays the way you want it. In the end, the grade itself should send water out of the bed and away from adjacent lawns or hardscape elements. This will help prevent any damage to those areas as well as keep your plants growing efficiently.

I genuinely believed at the start of my landscaping journey that my plants would still grow beautifully even if I didn't make my soil conditions optimal for that purpose. I was sure that I would at least see some results, but all that happened was me wasting time hoping for the best instead of taking time to do my best. Every step you take to prepare your site will affect the growth of your plants and the integrity of your hardscape structures.

Now that you've edged and graded your bed, it's time to add topsoil, compost, or a blend of the two to replace the soil you removed with the vegetation. The way you add soil to the bed depends on your region, soil type, and plant material. If you're not aware of these conditions, have a soil test done, and ask your local garden department about any further insight they can offer. This way, you won't waste your time placing plants that won't survive in your environment. In most cases, you'll be able to plant in the native soil, and add compost over the topsoil.

Preparing your site may feel like a challenge, especially if you are eager to get started on all of your projects.

You may want to rush the process, trying to get just enough debris out of your yard so you have a clean place to start, but ignoring other areas will just result in more work in the future. I didn't realize how long it would take to prepare my site, because going into it I thought I could get it done in a single day or at most a few days. While you could clear a single section and begin working on it, it will only result in more time wasted, because your design will have to be revised with every new encounter with your space. Take advantage of your preparation process, because it truly is just as important as the actual projects you're about to start.

Turning your outdoor space into an area you truly enjoy is an incredible experience. You've given yourself the blank slate you need to genuinely create a work of art out of your yard. You've cleaned, dug, assessed, and reevaluated every step you're going to take from this point on. Now you're ready to begin the projects that will slowly turn your barren landscape into a filled, flourishing environment that you'll be proud of.

4

INCORPORATING HARDSCAPE ELEMENTS

Before I learned what hardscape elements were, I assumed it referred to rough materials such as wood or stone, and I wasn't far off. Hardscape elements refer to parts of your landscape such as patios, decks, fences, walls, or walkways, that are solid, permanent, and immovable. They help shape your outdoor area and create some separation between your natural, or softscape, elements. A landscape needs to include both hardscape and softscape elements that work together in unison to create the ideal space.

Consider your ideal outdoor area, including the plans you've already devised. Where do you see these hardscape elements appearing and where will work best?

I imagined a majority of my hardscape elements close to the exterior of my home, such as my patio, outdoor kitchen, and entertaining area. Yet, I knew I wanted to see hardscape elements scattered throughout the rest of my landscape as well. It's only when you have the hardscape elements in place that you can see just where and how your plants, trees, or shrubs will fit in. Sometimes, when you start picturing your softscape elements in your landscape, you might find yourself having a hard time trying to figure out where they might go. That's because you haven't really begun laying down the foundation for these elements, and you may be lacking direction as well. The implementation of your hardscape elements will make that process a lot easier, and that's why it's best to tackle them before you move on to planting.

Depending on the size of your outdoor space, you might find yourself worrying about the cost of a project that includes an abundance of hardscape elements, but remember that you don't have to implement everything all at once. Prices can vary, and you can spread out the costs over time.

Everyone has a different idea of the kinds of elements they need to include in their spaces, and you may choose some of these items based on your budget or your current design. That is fine because all you need to remember is that you're building out this space to make you happy. Each hardscape element requires design, materials, and installation. That means that the prices are going to vary. According to *Homeadvisor.com*, here are a few prices to keep in mind:

- Concrete Patio: $2500
- Stamped Concrete: $4300
- Concrete Wall: $5000
- Deck: $7000
- Pathway: $3200

- Outdoor Kitchen: $9400
- Trellis, Pergola, or Arbor: $3500

These prices may seem rather high, especially if you've already set a budget to begin tackling your outdoor space on your own, but it's important to remember that you don't have to incorporate all your hardscape elements in one go. When I first began researching the elements I wanted to include, the prices themselves made me second-guess the entire process because I wasn't sure how I was going to make it work. But I realized that I could be building my outdoor space slowly, factoring each element into my budget comfortably without having to go overboard. You don't need to call in professionals to build your deck, outdoor kitchen, and patio all at once. Make improvements based on your own schedule and budget so you can enjoy your space without it feeling like a waste of money.

I started out with just a patio, building it out to my liking before I moved onto the next hardscape element a few weeks later. It took time, but it was certainly worth it because I ended up loving it, and I immediately knew it was worth the investment. Choose your elements wisely and you'll find that they're not as daunting you initially imagined.

The main landscape materials that you need to keep in mind are:

Wood and Faux Wood

Wood is generally the most popular hardscape material, but people often choose different options due to the fact that wood requires a great deal of maintenance. Wood isn't a great option for something like a walkway because the constant foot traffic will wear it down, and it will weather a lot faster than something like stone. You'll need to spend some time restoring, staining, and sealing your deck to avoid wear and tear over time, but if this is not something you're interested in doing, you may choose an entirely different material.

If you would rather go with faux wood, you'll get the appeal of wood without the constant weathering. Faux wood is made of composite hardscape materials, but makes it more expensive than natural wood. When you're deciding between the two, ask yourself just how much foot traffic will go through that area, because if it isn't a lot you may want to go with natural wood. If there will be, you might prefer faux wood. Think about the maintenance and how often you'd like to take care of this space because natural wood can also splinter during freezing weather conditions if not sealed properly. Natural wood is a more affordable option if faux wood is out of your budget.

Concrete

Concrete is a great material if you're looking for a cost-effective option that will last. In order for concrete to be installed, it needs to be formed, poured, finished, and cured correctly. Don't use concrete in spots where the ground might move, cave in, or crack over time. This will only result in expensive fixes that you want to avoid. Keep concrete away from softscape elements like trees or root systems that have problems draining because this could further damage them over time.

While concrete is a great option for those wanting to save money, it may not necessarily be the solution that fits your overall landscape design. Concrete needs to be cleaned regularly so you can prevent stains, grease, oil, mildew, or rust. You can expect cracks to occur over time and if this is going to disrupt your design then you might want to opt for a completely different material. You can typically patch or fill concrete cracks with products like a mix of epoxy and glue, but this might not be the seamless job you're looking for. A lot of people forego concrete due to how much it cracks and the maintenance required to keep it looking polished.

Asphalt

Asphalt is made from crushed rock with bitumen, which is a sticky petroleum byproduct. Asphalt will need to be well maintained, therefore you'll be spending some time keeping it clean of dirt, moss, and other debris that might damage it in the future. One of the biggest maintenance hurdles with asphalt is that it needs to be resealed every three to four years. You can use asphalt or tar-based products to repair any damage done to your asphalt areas, and these products typically have a warranty of 4-6 years.

You can mix and match hardscape materials as you wish, but it's important to keep in mind the kind of materials that will be the best fit for certain areas of your landscape so that you can minimize maintenance and maximize the time you get to enjoy your space.

Tile

Tile is a hardscape material that's usually quite expensive, and due to how specific the installation process needs to be, it's best left up to professionals. Trying to lay tile yourself might be too difficult a task to get done, especially considering all of the other work you'd still need to do in order to get your landscape looking the way you'd like. Tile is one of those materials that make an incredible addition to any space, even if it's just a small amount. Depending on what you choose and where you choose to include it, it can genuinely brighten up your entire outdoor area.

You have to ensure that you're choosing tile that can withstand outdoor weather conditions, because others simply won't hold up, and you'll find yourself having to replace them far too often. Keep in mind that your outdoor tiles need to be properly sealed to protect them from any damage that typical outdoor activity can cause. Whether you're using tile to dress up your outdoor kitchen or dining area, adding some interest to your seating area, or any other section you'd like to include it in, it's a good choice to have.

Bricks and Pavers

Bricks and pavers are the classic way to go when it comes to dressing up your outdoor area, adding visual appeal, and truly making a statement. They're both quite durable and that means they're going to last longer than other materials on this list. Your bricks and pavers can be mortared into place, laid onto the sand, or spread onto crushed rock. You should be inspecting your bricks and pavers regularly to ensure that there isn't any broken or loose mortar. If you notice any loose paving units, you should get them replaced right away because an uneven surface can cause injury. Brick, like stone varieties, will never truly lay flat, and that's something to keep in mind when it comes to deciding where you should best include it.

Remove any mildew, moss, or algae in any spaces that have a considerable amount of shade. If you have an area that becomes displaced, you can easily level them again using sand. When choosing the kind of brick that would best fit your space, you have a variety of textures and colors to choose from. Bricks themselves are made of clay and here are a few of the options you can look into if you'd like to include them in your space:

- Concrete bricks are a great option if you're looking for a cost-effective alternative but they tend to have a coarse finish even though they do maintain some balance when used in landscape design.
- There are common building bricks that are generally made of clay and used for the inner layers of brick walls. This really isn't a long-lasting choice if you'd like to include them on an outdoor path or patio.
- You may opt for face bricks which are usually higher quality and they have smooth faces. This makes resisting wear and tear a lot easier.

Bricks are generally graded by their ability to withstand different weather conditions.

- SW: Withstands severe weather conditions and performs well below freezing.
- MW: Withstands freezing as well as dry climates.
- NW: Doesn't withstand freezing but can withstand low rainfall.

Flagstone and Rock

Flagstone and rock are great options for an outdoor patio space. You may opt for either flagstone or bluestone when deciding on the right material for your patio, and it generally works best set in mortar, but you can also have it bedded in sand or crushed rock. This is a relatively low-maintenance material choice that may just require some light sweeping or washing every so often. Your patio area will see a lot of foot traffic, so having a material that can withstand weathering is very important.

You may want to choose something that's a bit less expensive than flagstone for your patio, and a great choice would be concrete pavers. They're made in different patterns which line up together for stability purposes. You can lay these quickly or on a flat surface which makes it a much easier process to complete.

Another great option is to use rock as one of your important materials in your landscape design. You can use crushed rock for your patio or walkway, but this will require a stable, rigid border to ensure that the crushed rock stays in place. This is a much better alternative to gravel because it makes walking a lot easier due to the irregular edges that lock together. If you've ever walked on gravel you remember the feeling of it rolling under your foot, and sometimes this can be an unpleasant experience!

Now that you have an idea of the kind of materials you can include as a part of your hardscaping projects, you may have a better idea of how to formulate your budget. Setting a budget can be challenging, but having a clear plan will help you make progress on your projects without sacrificing too much money at the beginning. Having an idea of the direction you're going in before you pay for anything will save you a lot of trouble in the long run.

Sometimes, we don't have enough time or money to offer up at the start of a project as big as this one, and that's perfectly fine. Figure out what's going to work best for you, and what will make budgeting for your landscaping projects easier on your wallet as well as your mind.

Measure your property so you'll be able to have a better idea of how many elements you're really going to need to fill the space. If your space is relatively small, you might be able to splurge on certain items since you won't have as much trouble building out the entire area. If you've got a lot of ground to cover, you'll need to factor a lot more into your budget for elements that will truly work well together in your landscape. You can also tackle your landscape by breaking it up into certain sections, focusing on a single zone at a time so that you'll be able to concentrate on your budget while making progress. You may want to tackle your patio or outdoor kitchen space first, or you may prefer to work on your outdoor seating area.

The one thing you need to remember is that your hardscape elements need to be laid out first before you begin spending time on your softscape elements. That's because it's going to be much harder to do it the other way around, and it can cause your space to look messy instead of clean.

What I found worked best for me was to break my landscape up into sections and focus solely on the hardscape elements for each before I moved onto the softscapes. Even if I did finish my walkway or patio space, I didn't immediately jump into working on my garden even though I had an idea of where it was going to go because I knew that could change over time. Instead, I took the time to finish all of my hardscape projects and then allowed myself to ease into the planting so that it wouldn't feel like too much work. This approach will be good if you're looking to take things slow, factoring in your budget, and starting small with the hardscape elements you're trying to incorporate into your space.

One thing people often fail to consider in their landscape design is the possible drainage issues you might encounter in the placing of your hardscape elements. Think about how water is going to drain effectively before you begin laying down your hardscape elements such as walls or spending your time working out the details of your patio.

You may want to consider contacting an independent landscape designer to best work out these issues, and even though that may be another upfront cost you'll have to think about, it may just save you a lot of time and money in the long run. The thought of having to deal with ruined plants or eroded hardscape elements might be one of the most frustrating things about landscape design, but if you work to ensure these issues never surface, you'll have a much better chance of keeping everything well-maintained. An independent designer will help you plan water runoff in an environmentally friendly and productive way. The one thing you're looking for is efficiency, because without that you're going to be doing a lot more heavy lifting than you bargained for.

An independent designer may suggest that you create a system that will help with drainage, one that will take all of the guesswork out of the process so you'll have more time to focus on other areas of your landscape that need your attention. This system could capture water for use throughout your landscape rather than simply implementing a drainage pipe to lead it out of your outdoor area entirely.

The next thing you're going to want to consider especially in regard to your hardscape elements is the shapes and transitions that occur throughout your space. I used to believe that I could include any shape I'd like or mix and match, only to find out that I was causing more obstruction throughout the flow of my landscape than adding visual interest to it. Depending on the style you're trying to go for, you may be more inclined to include more straightforward, linear shapes, or softer ones, but it's best to have a balanced mix of them both. Even though one may stay at the forefront of your entire design, creating continuity, you have to ensure that your space doesn't feel dull or too repetitive as you add similar items.

Repetition can be a great way to add a formal feel to your landscape, but if it's overused, it causes the space to look too uniform. You want a warm, inviting space that you're going to enjoy entirely, and you can accomplish that by finding the balance that's going to work best for you and your outdoor space.

A great way to avoid using too many of the same kinds of element is to play up the natural lines of the space, and add to it without taking away from the beauty that's already present. Remember, an overwhelming space is just one that's eventually going to be underused, and that is not what you're aiming for. Even if you've decided to go for a more formal landscape that includes a lot of linear elements, breaking these up with some curved shapes will help create balance. This way, your hardscape elements can blend into the space instead of coming off as harsh or out of place.

Choose materials for your space that compliment your style as well as the natural elements that are already in your space. During the period where you were clearing out your landscape, preparing it for your design, you presumably left the elements that made sense to you in the space, and these are what you're going to focus on as you start building out each individual section. You don't need to go with a single material in order to create a clean, balanced space. It's best to choose a few different materials that complement your style as well as give a variety of textures so the overall landscape itself is pleasing to the eye.

It's best to stick to at least two textures because too many will just make the space look messy or crowded. When you're starting these hardscape projects, buy more material than you need, because it's much easier to return than to keep heading back to the store whenever you realize that you need more. You can also make good use of any extra material you may have by creating accents throughout your space. You may even want to keep some on hand so that you can fix any damaged sections over time.

Now that you learned a great deal about hardscape elements as well as how to best incorporate them into your space, we will consider softscape elements, which are your plants. Your plants will brighten up your space and genuinely bring it to life, and that's why you need to plan what you're going to include as well as what purpose each of them is going to serve in your space.

5

ALL ABOUT PLANTS

Plants are the natural elements that will bring color and interest into your landscape. The inclusion of plants in your landscape allows you to enjoy your outdoor space, take in the fresh air, and even help you to maintain a healthy diet. When it comes to the kind of plants to include, you have to ask yourself what goals you want the garden sections of your landscape to serve. You may have already thought of planting a few nice flowerbeds or some shrubs, but what about a vegetable garden? A lot of the time, people tend to move away from including too many plants in their gardens because they're convinced that they will be too difficult to maintain. The best way to ensure that the plants you choose work well for your space as well as your upkeep schedule, is to learn more about them before you take the time to plant them in the ground.

The first plant category to consider is foundation plants. These are the beds of plants that create a border around your home, framing it, and generally consist of three parts. These are:

- Plants to line the entryway of your home.
- Plants that sit around the corners which act as a frame around your property.
- Plants that bridge the gap between the entryway and corner plants.

Not all plant beds in a landscape have all of these parts, but it's the starting point for a lot of people who want to incorporate more natural elements into their space.

While having sections throughout your backyard is important to both its appeal and functionality, incorporating these foundational elements throughout the rest of your landscape has benefits as well. Here are just a few:

- Plants such as shrubs are usually placed to hide raised concrete and they soften the harsh lines of the exterior of the house.
- If you don't have plants scattered across the entirety of your landscape, it could look barren or empty.
- When you're working with a small space, foundation plants provide extra room for additional plants because they create focal points for your garden areas.
- If you choose to include evergreen shrubs along the border of your home, this can decrease your heating cost by creating insulation around your home's foundation.

When you choose your plants, think of them at their mature height. You don't want to find yourself having to deal with plants that become too tall for your liking or obstruct your view, especially around your home.

Living Walls

You may want to create some separation between the softscape elements in your space, or continue to frame certain areas so that they're more closed off than others. You can achieve this by incorporating living walls into your landscape. The two main types of living walls are trees or shrubs. Trees are usually moderately priced, but take quite a long time to grow. They also need to be planted close together, but away from other elements that they might obstruct. Trees can often create root competition between adjacent plants, or they might cause further disruption of structures or utilities. You have to ensure that you're choosing the right places to plant your trees because if they're too close to your home or other buildings on your property, they could cause damage or injury in severe weather. This is something you should keep in mind while deciding how many trees to include as well as where they should go.

Another thing you need to consider while planting trees is that they're going to offer a considerable amount of shade. This can either be a good thing or a bad thing for your plants depending on how much shade they will need to thrive. The shade from trees can also impact the functionality of your yard as well as your neighbor's depending on how tall they are when they reach full maturity. Trees tend to have overhanging branches which can break off over time, falling around your yard, or your neighbor's. If you're not interested in spending the time trimming them down when they start to become a little overgrown, you may opt out of including too many around your property to avoid the maintenance. However, it's a great rule of thumb to include at least one or two trees on your property if you have the space for it because it does add quite a bit of visual interest.

The next category of softscape elements that can work as a living wall is shrubs. When you think of shrubs you might be thinking of the small ones that are scattered around your landscape to fill in space, but shrubs include a vast selection of tightly packed plants that can have a variety of different uses throughout your outdoor area. You can opt for hedges, which have a more structured form, or shrubs that are left alone to grow as they wish, which creates loose borders around your space, separating different sections without including too many straight lines.

You can use shrubs to create privacy screens throughout different areas of your landscape so that they can still blend together while maintaining separation so each zone doesn't feel too cluttered. This is especially useful for smaller spaces because it won't be as large as other hardscape privacy screens. Shrub walls or hedges can act just as effectively as hardscape walls if they have the right dimensions and they're placed in the right areas around your landscape. Living walls in general will require a lot more maintenance than hardscape walls, but they can be pleasing on the eye, and they may fit better into your space.

Consider the amount of sun these specific areas get along with the drainage they will need to thrive. Remember that as much as these natural elements act as walls in your space, they need to be well-maintained to flourish. Therefore, you should be checking on them just as much as you would your other plants. If you believe that a loose border would fit your landscape better, choose a mix of evergreen and deciduous shrubs. This will give you a variety of textures and create visual appeal. If you aren't limited on space, you may choose different sized shrubs to both fill and section off your outdoor area.

If your shrubs are going to be used as privacy screens then they need to be able to reach the desired density so that they can perform efficiently once they grow within the space. This is why you need to be aware of what the height and width these shrubs will be once they reach full maturity. A great tip for loose border shrubs is to keep them layered so that they reach their maximum potential at providing privacy as well as acting as a great natural element in your space. Place your tallest plants in the back and the shortest in the front while keeping shorter shrubs or tall perennials in the middle row. Your shortest plants should remain in the front, to create balance in your landscape.

When deciding on the best shrub choices for your landscape design, take into account the form of the shrub, the texture of its foliage or bark, and how it provides its color. Is it rich with greenery due to its leaves or does it have an abundance of flowers that provide some contrast?

Living walls are only one way to use plants in your softscape. Other kinds of plants can have a significant effect on your overall vision for your outdoor space.

Annuals

Annuals refer to the kind of plants that complete their entire life cycle throughout the course of a single season. Some examples of this may include: marigold, begonia, petunia, and nasturtium. You can use annuals to add different seasonal touches to your landscape, changing them out at the start of every new season to keep your space fresh. In hotter climates, annuals may not do as well, and this might lead you to decide on a different plant variety that will continue to bloom over a longer period of time.

Always remember to choose plants that fit your climate because if you try to incorporate too many that won't flourish, you will have to replace them far too often. If you take the time to remove the current blooms, this will allow your annuals to produce more vibrant blooms later on. Layer your annuals in three rows. The back row should be facing north if possible and should include your tallest plants. The middle row should have the next tallest varieties, and the front should have the shortest. Using repetition here is a great way to create continuity and bring certain areas of your space together, but remember that too much repetition can easily create a crowded, overwhelming space. Assess how your plants are going to look together before you put them in the ground and this will help you be sure of your decisions ahead of time.

Biennials

Biennials are less common than annuals or perennials and they usually live for about two years. Their first year they mainly produce foliage, and in their second, you'll see some flowering. Some flowering biennials include hollyhocks, foxglove, and canterbury bells. There are other biennials that aren't flowering, which are usually vegetables. They include brussels sprouts, carrots, beets, onions, leeks, celery, cabbage, and many others. Biennials will produce food within the first year, though they won't drop seeds or complete their growing cycles until the second season.

Perennials

Perennials are the plant that you'll want if you don't see yourself making any significant changes throughout the growth of your landscape. They typically live for more than two years, so when deciding on which ones to go with, ensure that they work well with the other elements in your space. Perennials are a great way to provide some vibrancy to your landscape alongside your annuals. While your perennials will last longer, switching out your annuals will help to create an entirely different look depending on the season.

Perennials remain in the ground all year round, and even though they die in the fall, they will sprout again the following season with new foliage as well as flowers. Some examples of perennials that you might want to consider for your space are anemone, dahlias, rudbeckia, hellebore, and salvia. A great way to add continuous color throughout your space is to plant a mix of both annuals and perennials so that you'll have some genuine visual interest in your space even after your perennials have bloomed.

Bulbs

Bulbs are some of the easiest plants to tackle, and they're a great starting point for any beginner. If this is your first time gardening at all, you may want to consider adding some bulbs to your space. Bulbs provide rich, vibrant color, and they also self-propagate so they'll spread quickly throughout the bed. That means you'll have a much easier time caring for them than you would other plants that struggle to thrive or that have longer growing periods. Some examples of bulbs that you can add to the garden sections of your landscape include tulips, daffodils, and hyacinths.

Evergreens

Evergreens are plants that retain their leaves year round. Your first thought with regard to evergreen plants may be trees, but there are quite a variety of evergreen plants to choose from apart from trees. They're great for adding color throughout different seasons, especially more barren ones like winter. Some examples of evergreen plants include holly and eucalyptus. There are some blooming shrubs that are considered to be evergreens because they retain their leaves year-round and they include laurels, azaleas, camellias, and gardenias.

Evergreens are a great option for foundation plants because they're great for framing areas of your home. Due to their ability to retain their leaves year-round, you won't have to experience time where your foundation plants have begun to wilt and that means your landscape will continue to flourish even during the change in weather conditions brought about by a shift in the seasons.

Deciduous

Deciduous plants are common, and you'll probably be able to recognize them easily because they're the kind that lose their leaves each year during the fall, remain barren throughout the winter, and begin to thrive again with a new canopy of leaves during the springtime. Deciduous plants generally require more maintenance than others because you're going to have to spend time cleaning up the fallen leaves and other debris every time they shed so that they don't disrupt other parts of your landscape. Some types of deciduous plants that you may want to consider incorporating into your outdoor area are birch trees, Japanese maple trees, and magnolias.

Vines

If you've included any wall-like elements, you may want some natural additions that will help balance the design itself and vines would be a great choice for this. Climbing plants will be perfect for your walls, fences, or archways. This will add some drama and interest to your landscape, playing up the natural feel of your other softscape elements while maintaining continuity. Most of the vines you'll come across are perennial, so they'll be back each year to bloom again. This will allow your structures to be covered in blooms, fruits, and leaves. Some vines you pick will be annuals, and that will help you decide how long you'd like them to be present as well as whether you'd like the opportunity to remove them once they've completed their growing cycles. Some vines include hops, morning glory, and clematis.

Vines can become invasive in your outdoor space if you're not careful. A lot of vines require so much maintenance that people often leave them out of their designs completely because they can't factor that amount of time into their personal upkeep schedules. You have to be sure about which vines you want to include, if any, and if you will be able to handle the maintenance so that they don't disrupt any of your other plants. I left vines out of my design specifically for this reason. The thought of having to deal with the overgrowth and vines crawling in all different directions when I wasn't there to take care of them made maintenance feel too much like a chore. So, leaving them out to focus on elements I actually wanted to see thriving in my space was the best way to go.

Ground Covers

Ground covers are a great way to take advantage of the horizontal space in your landscape. You've learned about a variety of plants that will help you take care of any blank space, reaching various heights to help you encourage balance, but have you given much thought to the plants that will remain rather short? Ground covers are low-growing plants, and that means they'll never reach significant heights.

After you've planted them, they'll form a dense mat along the ground to keep the weeds out. If you have any empty patches in your landscape that you're not sure what to do with, incorporating ground covers may be a great idea for you. Ground covers often produce beautiful flowers, and that allows you to control differing heights, take care of weeds, all while maintaining the overall visual interest of your landscape design. There are many varieties that you can choose from, but it's important that you're aware of each plant's needs before you put them into the ground. Some ground covers will need more sunlight than others, and that will require you to plant some away from the shade while others may need to be planted directly in it.

Ensuring that your ground covers have a chance to flourish and thrive will keep your landscape looking beautiful while keeping your upkeep process rather simple. Some examples of ground covers include thyme, bearberry, and bishop's weed.

Aquatic Plants

Are you planning on including any water features in your landscape design, such as a pond or another small body of water? Have you ever taken a look at one of these features and noticed that they're quite barren looking? That's because there aren't enough aquatic plants within them to bring them to life and make them look natural. Incorporating aquatic plants into your landscape design will ensure you're maintaining the natural feel of your design while choosing plants that will thrive in those spaces.

Aquatic plants purify and oxygenate the water while adding a special touch to your landscape design. They're a great addition for ponds with fish. Some aquatic plants include blue lotus, lemna, fairy moss, and water lilies.

Shrubs

You've learned quite a bit about shrubs already, but there are different varieties that you may come across and different purposes shrubs may serve in different areas of your landscape. Shrubs consist of both deciduous and evergreen plants. They're dense, compact, and they bring color and texture to your outdoor area. They don't have to be an addition you solely keep to your garden spaces, because they can add visual appeal at just about any corner of your landscape, even the most barren ones.

You're already aware that shrubs make great foundation plants, but they also are great for different gardening techniques. The one thing you need to keep in mind when planting and caring for shrubs is they need a trim every so often to keep their structured look unless you're trying to go for more of a natural texture with the ones you choose. Some examples of shrubs include viburnum, azaleas, and lilacs.

Grasses, Rushes, and Sedges

Grasses, rushes, and sedges are usually referred to as ornamental grasses, and each one comes from a different plant family. Each family of ornamental grasses has their own requirements for care, such as different needs for sun and moisture. These can be challenging to deal with as a gardener.. Some people leave them out and try to liven up the grass they already have available to them. If you feel that ornamental grasses are perfect for your specific space, there are a few things to keep in mind.

You can differentiate between these grasses by looking at the stems. Grass stems are usually round and hollow while rush stems are round and flat. Sedge stems are a triangular shape. No matter which kind of grass variety you choose, ensure that they're receiving full sun and the soil is well-drained. Sedges are generally used for damp, shady environments, but the category that thrives the best in wet areas are rushes. They're generally found alongside the edge of a body of water. Some of these grasses include bamboo and lake sedge.

Cacti and Succulents

Cacti and succulents are great plants to retain moisture, as they store water in their leaves, stems, and roots. This allows them to thrive in the hottest of landscapes, and if you currently live in an environment where you don't get many seasonal changes, these might be great additions to your outdoor area. Cacti and succulents are ideal for desert landscapes and they're relatively low-maintenance, which means you'll have a much easier time caring for them over the course of their growing cycles. The requirements for cacti and succulents to truly thrive are loose sandy soil, infrequent rain, and hot temperatures year-round. Some examples of these are aloe vera and asparagus.

Tropical

Tropical plants have a distinct look to them, and they display a lot of exotic colors and textures that you don't find in other plants. Tropical plants have very specific flowering patterns, and they can be a great addition to your landscape if you live in an environment where they're going to be able to thrive well. Most tropical plants are no longer hardy past zone 8. Some tropical plants include palm trees and tiger claws.

THINGS TO CONSIDER WHEN CHOOSING YOUR PLANTS

There are a few considerations to keep in mind when you're choosing your different plant varieties. When you're deciding on the kinds of trees you're going to incorporate into your outdoor area, remember that they're incredibly slow growers. That means you're going to have to be sure of their position and what they're going to look like at full maturity, otherwise you'll risk throwing off your entire landscape design. Also take into account branch reach and root systems when you're planning the placement of your trees.

A great rule of thumb is to plant your deciduous trees to the south and west of your home so you can take advantage of the shade they offer. This will help to reduce your air conditioning costs during the summer months. Since they will drop leaves in the winter, you'll still be able to get a considerable amount of sunlight when you need it. Plant your evergreen trees to the north and west of your home to act as windbreaks.

Invasive Plants

When you're starting your gardening journey, you may encounter a variety of invasive plants, including some that you may have chosen for your landscaping. A lot of people don't realize how invasive the plants they choose are until they start disrupting other plants in the surrounding area, ruining all their hard work. Taking the time to learn about the different characteristics of invasive plants will help you as you begin to get more comfortable with gardening itself.

Invasive plants refer to ones that grow where you don't want them to, and that makes them difficult to control. Different environmental conditions have different invasive plants that could become a problem in your space, so research to see which you'll need to avoid so you can make your landscaping process as easy as possible. Some plants might be invasive during the warmer months, but not as much in the winter. There were quite a few times where I included some invasive plants in my garden space, only to realize what I'd done far too late, and having to do damage control was a very difficult and frustrating process.

YOUR CLIMATE AND YOUR GARDEN

You can utilize a zone map to better pinpoint the kinds of plants that would be a good fit for where you live. Looking up your current zone and the conditions associated with it such as moisture and soil content will help you plant a garden that will flourish. In the U.S., they are sectioned into thirteen different zones that are referred to as USDA zones. Each zone covers a 10 degree range. Here's an overview of two zones so you can get a better idea of where you may fit:

- Zone 1: This zone is the coldest with a minimum winter temperature of -60 to -50 degrees Fahrenheit.
- Zone 13: This zone has a minimum winter temperature of 60 to 70 degrees Fahrenheit.

If you're anything like me, there was a time where you weren't sure whether your environment conditions would really have that much of an effect on your plants, and I'm here to tell you that they will. You don't want to have to dig out the plants you just placed into the ground because you chose ones that wouldn't be able to survive in your current weather conditions. Learn about the conditions your plants need to thrive and build a garden that will make you happy, while ensuring that your hard work pays off.

One more thing that you need to be aware of with regard to your plants is their hardiness. Plant hardiness refers to their ability to survive during severe weather conditions, like flooding, drought, heat, or cold. Your plants' genetics determine their ability to withstand these conditions, and that means they will require very specific environments to thrive. This may mean that you'll have to skip out on including a few plants that may have caught your eye if they're not a great fit for your current environment, but it's better than watching them wilt far too quickly.

When your plant is hardy to a specific zone, it will generally thrive well at any zone number that's higher. For example, most plants that are hardy to zone 3 will thrive in zone 7 as long as it meets their requirements.

6

OVERCOMING CHALLENGES

Throughout your landscaping and gardening journey, you will face some challenges that might disrupt the flow of your progress, but that's never a reason to give up. If I had listened to the doubt and worry that I wasn't going to be able to pull my landscaping projects off, I wouldn't have ended up with such a beautiful outdoor area where my family and I get to spend a great portion of each day with each other. You may be trying to brush up on all the possible problems that might occur so that you won't run into any issues once you actually begin the work, but chances are you're still going to find something that will be a bit difficult to overcome. I'm going to walk you through those possible problems so you do feel prepared, and even though things may become a little challenging, there's always a way to make it through.

No matter how good of a plan you have at the beginning or how long you've been working out the details of the projects you'll be tackling, something will always come up. There were times in my own landscaping journey where I second-guessed my abilities, or convinced myself that I wasn't capable of continuing because I'd already made so many mistakes. Once I was able to move past that, I began looking for ways to work around the problems and do what was necessary so I didn't end up with an outdoor area I'd never use.

I've seen many people simply decide to live with the mistakes they made in their design instead of finding ways to change them, because of their budget constraints or the work it was going to take. Remember, your ultimate goal is to create a space that you're going to enjoy, and that may mean that you'll have to modify some of your choices or spend a little more than you initially thought. You don't have to work through all of your challenges at the same time. If you find an issue in your landscape design, take a deep breath, assess the problem, and find the suitable solution. For some problems, this may mean handling it all on your own, and for others you may need some professional help. Don't be afraid to reach out if you need to because it may just save you a great deal of time and effort in the long run.

DRAINAGE ISSUES

One common problem you're going to have to look out for is drainage issues. There are three main categories of drainage issues that you may come across (LandscapingNetwork.com):

- **Surface Water:** If your yard has clay-based soil, you may encounter problems with lingering surface water which causes muddy areas throughout your yard. The solution to this problem is to incorporate surface drainage. You can utilize a French drain, which is a trench that's filled with gravel that has roofing, felt, or geotextiles over the top with the soil replaced. The area surrounding this will drain to this trench so the water doesn't linger on the surface, which will minimize damage done to your landscape.

- **Hardpan:** This refers to a cemented layer within the soil that's caused by lime, iron, or silicate materials depositing and cementing the soil particles together (Copernicus.com). If you have any hardpan layers throughout your landscape, this can cause poor drainage and standing water which will affect the growth of your plants as well as damage other elements you may have. A solution for hardpan layers is site-wide grading and installation of trench drains as well as a pipe system so the water will effectively flow out.
- **High Water Table:** If your landscape has any low-lying areas that suffer from your location on a high water table, it can make landscaping feel like a challenge. This is because your plant roots are saturated during the growing season and they are denied oxygen. This will lead to your plants quickly rotting, and it will ruin all the hard work you've put into your garden

space. A solution for high water table issues is to pick plants that do well in high water landscapes like riparian species from local bogs, fens, and swamps. Another solution is to raise the planting areas or opt for container gardening instead of laying your plants directly in the soil. If you're planting limited shrubs and perennials, your planter will be far more shallow and less expensive than ones needed for trees and larger shrubs. You can do this with or without the help of a designer depending on the different plants you choose and the conditions the plants will survive in.

HOT CLIMATE ISSUES

If you live in an area that gets a lot of sun, you might run into some problems along the way. A lot of people equate warmer climates with better growing conditions, but this isn't always the case. If your landscape is fully exposed to the west, the heat of the day can put a strain on your plants. Whether you're dealing with hot, dry, humid, or a mix of them all, your conditions dictate how your plants will thrive and whether or not they're going to flourish.

There are a few seasonal solutions that you can choose to make the process of dealing with exceptionally warm, humid climates easier. The first solution is the use of tensioned fabric structures and shade sails. Shade sails are an appealing and effective solution that can be quick to install, and they can help you deal with an intense amount of heat. Shade sails can be purchased in many different colors and sizes. Many companies will custom make them to fit the dimensions of your garden or yard. These sails usually involve steel poles, cables, and turnbuckles. You may be able to complete the installation of these sails yourself, but in some instances it's best to reach out for professional help to ensure that it's done correctly. You can also look into including retractable awnings, especially over your patio areas, so you can enjoy your space even when it's hot and humid.

Other structures can provide the same amount of shade while offering different looks that may better fit with your overall design. You can incorporate shade structures with beams or rafters that run overhead in a section of your landscape to keep those areas cool or you can look into installing a prefabricated pergola. This is a freestanding flat-top structure that will provide a great deal of protection from the sun. Kits for pergolas are available in a variety of materials, and choosing the right one will depend on the look you're going for as well as your budget. You can choose from materials like wood, steel, or vinyl. You may be looking at spending $1200 to $1700 which doesn't include shipping or installation. While this may be an expensive purchase, it can truly help with heat issues that might end up ruining your landscape in the long run.

Another shade option that also acts as a natural softscape element is a tree. A large tree is a green and sustainable solution for heat or sun issues you may have, but you won't be able to plant them too close to your home due to root or branch damage they may cause. Remember, in regards to installing for shade purposes, you're going to need a licensed landscape architect to select the right one and take care of installation so you can transplant with ease. The biggest challenges that you're going to come across have to do with the cost and accessibility. While you can plant trees on your own, choosing the right one that will provide the shade you need can be tricky. You also have to consider that trees are slow growers so if you're looking for shade right away, having one transplanted is your best option. Though, that will require some professional landscaping help to get the job done effectively. You also may want to look into plants that are going to thrive in the sun such as blue agave, tropicanna, orchid rockrose, and Texas ranger.

EYESORES AND OTHER ISSUES

Take a good look around your landscape and pinpoint any eyesores you may see. This can include elements such as a bulky air conditioning unit or a propane tank. Items such as barbecue grills won't be much of a problem because you're not exactly trying to hide it like you are with these other items. The goal should be to create some separation between these large items and the rest of the space. A solution for hiding bigger items such as these is to place tall, slender shrubs next to them. This will soften the harsh lines they give your landscape and break up the space while adding additional foliage.

Air conditioning units themselves require at least 2-3 feet of room around them so the air can circulate effectively, and so the exhaust works well. You can use a cluster of plants in front of and around air conditioning units, taking into consideration the space they need between the shrubs and the units themselves. Plants that have finely textured leaves will fade into the background, and you can use these in addition to plants with bigger foliage to create depth. This will help you turn those eyesores into beautifully full, flourishing garden spaces while ensuring that they remain well-maintained and practical. Your goal is to draw the eye away from unattractive items like these, with the help of the natural elements.

Another problem to avoid is erosion and runoff. Runoff carries pollutants to bodies of water, depositing sediment, and this will increase your water bill. An effective solution for this is to install artificial grass on sloping ground to ensure proper drainage. A solution to prevent erosion on an area like a driveway is to install pavers.

While you continue your gardening journey, you might find some difficulty growing plants in the shade. Shade gardens are generally used to incorporate plants that don't require as much sunlight as others, and they usually only need it during certain times of the day. Evaluate the degree of the shade before you place any plants into the ground so that you can avoid them struggling to grow. A solution for this would be to plant flowers and herbs that thrive in shade areas, so you can encourage growth as well as greenery without the need for direct sunlight.

ASSESSING YOUR PROGRESS

During the different stages of your landscaping journey, you may want to take the time to assess how you're progressing with your original plan. If something feels off or looks like it may cause damage to your plants or other elements, do some research and correct those issues before they have a chance to get worse. When I first started my landscaping journey I came across a variety of issues that I've already listed and some that were a big deal at the time until I took a step back, figured out a solution, and kept working toward my goals.

Like any process in life, landscaping is going to take time, and there will be many instances when things simply won't go your way. Working around certain problems that surface and figuring out the right solutions is a significant part of the landscaping process, especially when you know that it doesn't just end when you finally have your outdoor area looking the way you want it to. The maintenance and upkeep alone means that you're going to have to be checking in on various sections of your landscape to ensure that everything remains in working order. If you don't, you're more likely going to find many more problems in the future. It's true when people say that a landscape can become overgrown or difficult to manage when you don't take the time to care for it.

Think back to the plan you made for your landscape in the earlier chapters. Look over how far you've come, all of the elements you've already installed, the plants that have begun to grow, and think about the direction your landscape is going to take now. Don't be afraid to make changes, because at the end of the day, if you don't like it, you're never going to get the best use out of your space. The only way to overcome your obstacles is to continue to practice, learn, and take action. This is your opportunity to change the entire outcome of your landscape and prepare for the projects that will completely transform your outdoor space.

7

PROJECTS TO GET YOU STARTED

If you're still unsure of how to begin your landscaping design projects, I'm going to walk you through a few that will make the process itself a lot easier. When I first started, I had no idea how to see my projects through, because I allowed myself to get sidetracked or I tried to accomplish too many things all at once. The best way to ensure that you're making consistent progress and maximizing your time is to complete one project before moving on to the next. In the midst of being overwhelmed and excited, you might find yourself wanting to jump from one project to the next, but this is only going to make things more difficult for you in the long run. Let's start with one of the more simple projects, building a flower bed.

HOW TO BUILD A FLOWER BED

First, mark the area you'd like your flower bed to sit. You can use white flour or brightly colored paint to do this, but marking it out will help you visualize exactly where it needs to go. Don't be afraid to do this a few times until you have it at the right place, because it'll be difficult to move it around later on.

The next step requires you to remove the grass within the lines. Your lines are going to act as the border for your bed, and it's best that you don't remove the grass too far outside this border so you can keep everything looking clean. There are two ways to remove the grass. The first requires you to do some digging, so you can use a shovel to remove the existing sections of grass from the center of your bed, then you can continue to remove the turf by wedging your shovel under the edges of the grass. It's best that you dig at least 4-5 inches around the bed's perimeter. Once you've done that you can lift and peel the sod away. Afterward, ensure that you clean up any debris that's left behind and loosen the soil while working in some organic matter like fertilizers.

If you'd prefer not to dig, you can approach this without having to grab your shovel. First you're going to want to cover the area of your planned flower bed with at least six pages of newspaper, overlapping as you go. Next, cover the newspaper with a few inches of soil or compost and water it well. Over the course of the next few months the grass underneath the newspaper will die and the newspaper will decompose, which will add nutrients to the soil. This will allow you to build a flower bed over time if you're not looking to get it done immediately.

HOW TO BUILD A RAISED FLOWER BED

Building raised flower beds is a great way to take advantage of space that doesn't have any soil because you're going to be able to add your own. This is great especially if you're dealing with small spaces because you may not have enough natural soil space to plant your flowers in. To start, you'll need to create a four-sided structure using lumber that has been cut to your desired length. A great rule of thumb is to keep your raised garden bed four feet deep or less. If you were to make it any wider than this, it can be difficult to reach the center of the bed when it comes time to plant or care for your flowers. Next, place the shorter walls up against the longer ones and create a rectangle. Attach these by drilling pilot holes and using 2 ½ inch deck screws. Once both your short and long walls are attached, you're ready to begin laying your soil and planting.

HOW TO BUILD A SIMPLE WOOD-BURNING FIRE PIT

A wood-burning fire pit is a great addition to any outdoor space because it truly elevates your entertaining atmosphere. It's great especially on chillier nights when you're spending time with your friends and family. To begin, mark the outer diameter with a brightly colored spray paint. Next, remove any sod, stone, roots, or any other debris from inside the circle. Dig into the circle at least five inches deep, but make sure the circle itself is level. Fill the fire pit with gravel, level it, and tamp down. Grab your fire pit pavers and lay them on top of the gravel before placing the steel ring in the center. Now, grab your fire pit stones and lay them around the ring, overlapping a few of them. You're going to need to secure your stones onto the fire ring with a rubber mallet. If you still think that they're going to move around, you may want to add a little adhesive to keep the stones in place so you'll feel safe knowing that they're snug.

HOW TO BUILD A SIMPLE PATIO

A patio space is one of the most important parts of your entire landscape. It's the area where you're probably going to spend the majority of your time, and the ways in which you can use this space are truly endless. You may want to include an outdoor dining area or an outdoor kitchen where you'll be able to utilize your barbecue grill during the summer. If you currently do not have a patio space, here are the steps to build one out yourself.

The materials you need are:

- Shovel
- Pavers
- Landscape Fabrics
- Sand
- Class 5 Crushed Concrete or Gravel

- Plastic or Aluminum Edging
- Rubber Mallet
- Stakes

Check with your local utility company that there are no buried water, gas, or electrical lines on your property because these can be very dangerous if ignored. Once you've done that, you can start on your patio prep. The height of the patio once it's finished will be slightly above the surrounding ground so that you won't have any lingering water on the surface.

Start by digging down and leveling the surface so that you can create a foundation. Wetter soil will need a thicker base than soils that have appropriate drainage. You can use landscape fabric to reinforce the area beneath the pavers so it'll be stable. This will also allow water to flow freely through the soil.

Fill your entire area in with at least four inches of Class 5 gravel, as well as a choice between gravel and sand. Tamp it down so the area stays smooth. Once you've done that, it's time to install your paver border using plastic or aluminum edging, and secure it with your stakes. Lay the pavers and tap them down firmly so they're secure by using a rubber mallet. This will help them settle into the sand. If you have any cracks in your sand, you can add more sand to the top to fill them in.

If you're not sure about the size that you want, always opt for a bigger size because it will be far more difficult to make a stone patio bigger later on.

HOW TO EDGE A GARDEN BED WITH BRICKS, PAVERS, OR STONES

Edging a garden bed with bricks, pavers, or stones can genuinely enrich your landscape space and add depth to each garden section. The materials for this project are:

- Bricks, stones, and pavers
- Rope
- Circular Saw
- Tape Measure
- Marker
- Spade

Your first step will be to create a route for brick edging. Use the rope as a guide around your planting bed so you can better determine where your brick edging will go. Mark where you'll be cutting the rope and be sure that the rope itself follows the curves while staying above the grass line. You can use a tape measure if you have trouble finding the exact length. Divide the length in inches by 4 or by the width of the brick tack. Next, add a few bricks or pavers to determine how deep the trench needs to be. If you're using stones instead you have to place them at least 3 inches thick and 4 inches wide so the grass won't grow up through them.

Ensure that you've filled the gaps before you begin digging the trench. Dig a trench a bit wider than the length of the bricks. Check to ensure that the sides of your trench are straight. The paver itself should be at least 6 inches deep so that it sits firmly on the ground. Next all you need to do is spread the paver base and cement mixture. Then, it'll be time to lay your bricks.

HOW TO INSTALL A WALKWAY

Walkways are absolutely necessary for your landscape because they help guide you through the entire area. Without them creating some separation between your elements and different zones, your landscape might look messy or overgrown. The materials that you need to install a walkway are:

- Pressure-Treated 2x4s
- Crushed Limestone
- Bricks
- Sand
- Landscaping Fabric
- Marking Paint

- Rake
- Hammer
- Metal Edging with Stakes
- Brick Tongs
- Wet Saw
- Measuring Tape

Remove any existing pavers and ensure that you've cut your plants down and removed any roots. Once you've done that, mark the outline for where you'd like your walkway to go. You can use a transfer shovel to remove any loose rock before you get ready to tamp down the soil you've turned up from the digging. Make sure that you've filled and smoothed out any indentations. Now it's time to lay the landscaping fabric. Using a rake, spread your crushed limestone paver base to a depth of 4" to 6". Insert your metal edging along the sides of the walkway and secure them with your stakes.

You're ready to apply your sand and bricks. Start by applying sand to the path by using the back of a rake. Ensure that it's consistent and that you've tamped it down. Start laying your bricks around the border, tapping each one into place with your rubber mallet. Use your screed to level the sand. Once you've got all your bricks laid out, pour sand over the top and rake the entire walkway. Then, using a broom, sweep across the entire path. This way you'll be sure to get every crevice.

HOW TO CREATE A POND

Ponds and other water features are great to add a bit of nature back into your space to break up the greenery. Some may think that approaching the building of a pond may be too difficult a task, but it's very possible to add this lovely water element into your outdoor area. The materials you're going to need for this project are:

- Preformed Polyethylene Pond Liner
- Flexible PVC Pond Liner
- Pond Filter
- Pond Pump
- Pea Gravel
- All-Purpose Sand
- Egg Rock
- Brown River Rock
- Black Mexican Beach Pebbles
- Pond Tubing
- Mulch
- Stainless Steel Adjustable Hose Clamps
- Pond & Stone Spray Foam Insulation
- Marking Paint

Your first step is to place the preformed pond liner at the location you'd like your pond to be. Mark the location with your marking paint so you'll know exactly where it is as you begin working on the project itself. Now, move the liner you placed and begin digging out the area. Dig a few inches wider than what you marked and 3 inches deeper than the liner. This will help you avoid a pond that's too small, throwing off your entire landscape, especially the balance in the area where your pond is going to go. You'll need this space to add a layer of sand that will act as the base for the shell.

Remove any roots, rocks, or other debris you may find as you dig. Try to keep the hole as level as possible while you work. Place the liner in the hole. The top edge should be right at the ground level. You can check this by laying a straight 2x4 on the edge across the liner and place a level right over the board. Now, remove the liner so you can add at least three inches of sand to the hole. This will raise the edge of the pond a few inches above the ground.

Now you'll need to level out the sand you just placed with the back of a garden rake and place the liner. Place the 2x4 across the liner again to ensure you have a 2 to 3 inch gap between the liner and the ground. Check to make sure that the liner is level by placing the level on the 2x4. Now you can leave the 2x4 and the level where they are, pouring the sand into the hole to begin backfilling around the shell itself.

LOOKING AHEAD

You're at that point in your landscaping journey where you're genuinely trying to figure out whether the progress you've made thus far will continue as planned. You've learned about all the different elements that you can include, the projects you can start, and the mistakes that you may encounter. The question is now, how are you going to turn your current landscape into an absolute dream?

When I first started making progress on my own landscape, I found that I wanted to make a few changes quite early, and this made me have to abandon a few projects that I had already put a significant amount of time and effort into. It felt terrible having to leave them behind, but I knew that if I didn't make the changes, I would be stuck with an outdoor space I would never use. Some projects will be much easier than others, and some will seem far too difficult to even attempt. Remember, you can ask for professional help, even if you have already begun to attempt the process yourself.

There were times where I was convinced that I could take on projects that simply couldn't be completed by one person, hoping for the best even though I knew I should've hired out for those tasks. It wasn't until I was halfway through, almost ready to give up, that I realized I needed help to continue, otherwise I'd probably end up injuring myself or doing an unprofessional job. There were also times where I had debated trying to hire out the entire landscaping design itself because I worried I'd run into more trouble along the way, but I quickly began to see a change once I took a step back, reassessed my capabilities, and moved forward.

You may find yourself biting off a little more than you can chew, wanting to throw in the towel, and maybe even asking yourself whether designing a landscape is even the right way to go. I'm here to assure you that it certainly is. Imagine all of the time you could be spending outdoors, the vegetables you'd be able to grow, the warm summers that you can't wait to enjoy. Those are what make all of the work worth it, and even if you find yourself encountering a few obstacles along the way, that doesn't mean you should give up.

Landscaping is by no means an easy task. It takes time, effort, dedication, and basic understanding of the concepts necessary to do a good job. Remember, like any other process you'll come across in life, landscaping can be learned. Taking the time out of your day to make a little progress is much better than trying to get it all done at once or even leaving it unattended for far too long, not knowing how to continue when you eventually revisit it. You have the chance to change your landscape for the better.

If you're in the middle of your landscape design and you suddenly decide that things aren't moving in the direction you want, head back to the drawing board before you make any more progress on elements or additions that don't work like you thought they would. If you've decided that you do not want to include so many flower beds, or you'd rather use those areas for something else, don't be afraid to change things up. You can take the time to change your plan at any time during the process, especially if you feel like you've figured out a better option. The only thing I'd suggest is to try to nail your design before you begin planting because once you've got your seeds in the ground, it's going to be quite difficult moving them around or even swapping them out entirely. The same goes for any plants that have established roots because you have to be careful not to damage them during the transplanting process.

If you've begun working on a larger project such as a hardscape element only to find that you're not going to move in that direction after all, you may want to repurpose the materials for a project that's more fitting for your space. Modifying your plans can feel like a challenge, especially if you already had everything figured out, but it's worth it if it's going to make you love the end result more. This process itself took me out of my comfort zone and it filled me with a considerable amount of doubt, but once I finally started moving in the right direction for my space, I enjoyed the tasks that much more.

Once I threw myself into it, it no longer felt as daunting to set aside a little time every day to work on my landscaping projects, even though I had an already packed schedule. It was something I began looking forward to, and it was slowly beginning to change my life. Your landscape design will do so much more for you than you may even realize, and the best way to stick with it is to check in with yourself on your progress, assessing the direction you're moving in so you remain on track. Once you know you're building the landscape of your dreams, you'll be more inclined to move past your obstacles and get the job done.

LEAVE A 1-CLICK REVIEW!

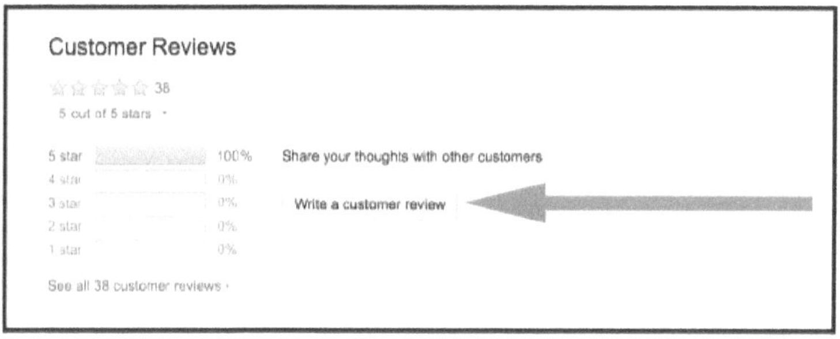
Customer Reviews
38
5 out of 5 stars
5 star
100%
4 star
0%
3 star
0%
2 star
0%
1 star
0%
See all 38 customer reviews
Share your thoughts with other customers
Write a customer review

I would be incredibly thankful if you could take just 60 seconds to write a brief review on Amazon, even if it's just a few sentences!

Scan the QR code below to leave a review!

LEAVE A REVIEW

CONCLUSION: CONTINUE YOUR LANDSCAPING JOURNEY

You've embarked on a journey that will transform your outdoor space into an area where you'll spend a considerable amount of time. You've assessed your yard, evaluated everything that is already there, so that you'll be able to make the changes necessary to turn it into your dream. You may already be envisioning all of the wonderful outdoor activities that you'll be able to do now that you're making good progress on your outdoor area.

It's time to look over that plan of yours one more time, check in on all the projects you're currently working on, and create a timeline that will help you see your projects through to the finish line. Right now, especially while you're doing a great deal of research as well as reading this book, you're feeling excited and very much inclined to make consistent progress on your landscape, but what's going to happen when life gets in the way? One of the biggest lessons I learned very early on in my landscaping journey is that trying to stick to too strict of a schedule will only result in the process itself feeling less rewarding. By forcing yourself to choose between your other responsibilities and this project, you're only going to feel the need to put it off even more. Finding the balance between getting your landscaping done and giving yourself room to relax is crucial. It helped me finish my landscape design and create a maintenance schedule that didn't feel overwhelming.

Landscaping isn't something that you can get done overnight. It's not going to happen in a few days even, unless you've got a large team of people coming in to transform it for you. Going at this relatively alone may seem difficult even after everything you've learned in the chapters in this book, but you'll be the one reaping the benefits at the end. If you were to leave everything in the hands of a designer, the chances of your landscape coming out the exact way you want it are slim. No one can know what you like better than you. Even if what you like changes over time, at least you've begun picking up the necessary skills to help you figure out how to make those modifications so you can continue to love your space.

CONCLUSION: CONTINUE YOUR LANDSCAPING JOUR... | 149

Even after having my finished landscape for a few years, I've still found myself wanting to move things around, and change the design elements I once loved so much. That's fine, because I've built a space that can evolve with me instead of relying on one that I'd have to keep the same because I have no idea how to go about changing it. The skills you've learned throughout the course of this book and in practice will be useful to you for the rest of your life. You may even opt to include your friends and family in the progress, which makes the finished product that much more memorable.

The best way to approach any landscaping project is to break it down and start with the simple tasks. You may want to jump right into the difficult things, allowing yourself to get too caught up in getting everything right, when you should be taking it all one step at a time. The simpler you keep both your process and the overall design of your landscape, the more you will like it in the end. Remember, overcrowding your landscape with too many elements especially if you have a smaller space to begin with, isn't the answer. It'll only leave you feeling cramped and wishing you had done things differently. Even if you like a fuller space, adding elements one by one, taking into account how they're going to look together will help you ensure that you like everything you incorporate into your space. While it can be easy to get carried away, you have to remember what your end goal is. You're creating the landscape you've always wanted, the one that will bring a little extra joy to your life, and for that to happen, make sure that every element you add has a reason to be there.

Throughout the rest of your landscaping journey, there's one thing to have to keep in mind, and that's the fact that nothing is ever really going to stay the same. Even if you've got yourself a finished landscape and you love the way it looks right now, things will look different over time. That's why it's important to take what you've learned from this book and apply it to your landscape design no matter how long you've been doing it. You'll be tending to your hardscape elements, caring for your plants, cleaning your outdoor furniture for as long as you enjoy your space, but you may decide one day that it needs another addition to be perfect to you. Now that you've begun learning more about the wonderful things you'll be able to accomplish in your outdoor space, you'll find true joy and happiness in completing the projects that are special to you.

You've created the plan and now it's time to put it into action. Remember, small efforts are where the wins are because once you're able to make them consistently, you'll be well on your way to designing and creating the landscape you've truly always wanted. You're the one that gets to make all of the decisions, deciding where things will go, and how things will look when it's finally all complete. Don't forget to have fun through each step of your landscaping journey, and relish the fact that you're building a space that will truly enrich the way you enjoy the outdoors.

CONNECT WITH US!

Don't miss out on our awesome community!

Scan the QR code below to join!

STAY UP TO DATE

Join our newsletter to stay up to date with all the latest tips, tricks and gardening hacks.

Don't miss out
Join now!

DON'T FORGET YOUR FREE GIFT!

Want to shovel your way to success?

Scan the QR code below to claim yours today!
Claim yours below!

SOURCES

CopernicusPSD.com. "What is Hardpan and How to Break It Up."

Gilmer, Maureen. "Solutions for Homesite Drainage." LandscapingNetwork.com.

Landscapemanagement.net. "Step by Step: How to Prep a Landscape Bed." January 11, 2016.

www.ingramcontent.com/pod-product-compliance
Lightning Source LLC
Chambersburg PA
CBHW030439010526
44118CB00011B/712